DISTURBING BEAUTY

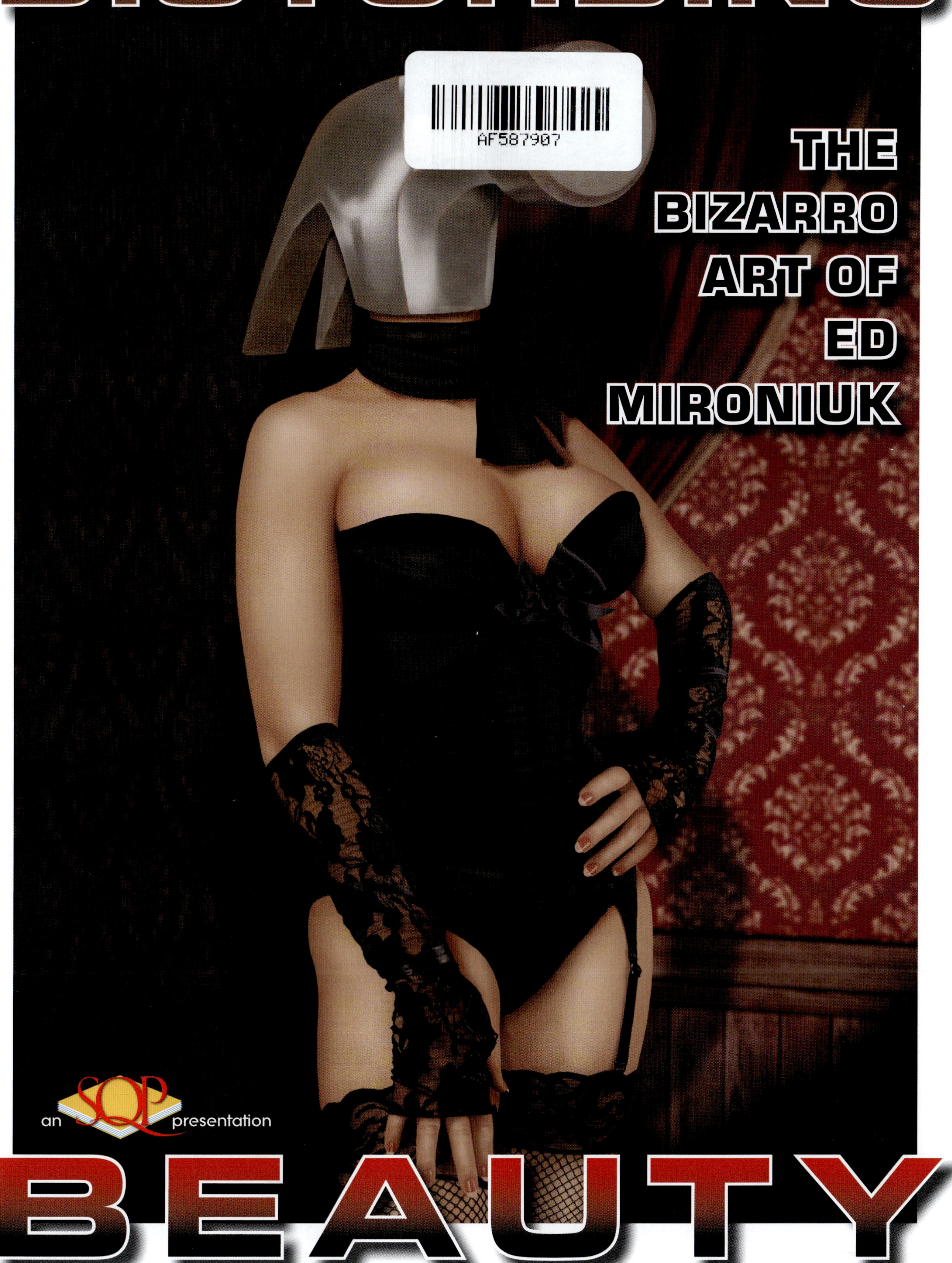

WELCOME TO BIZARRO WORLD

Ed Mironiuk makes the uncomfortable oddly comforting

When something is so wrong, it mysteriously becomes so right. This is the disreputable playground that artist and damaged prophet Ed Mironiuk lords over with unabashed glee. Armed to his sharpened teeth with a twisted sense of gallows humor and a glorious jaundiced eye for illustration - the resulting paintings are a sour/sweet treat for the eye and the brain (and assorted other bodily organs.)

This collection includes many cover paintings done for a series of books by the renown author Carlton Mellick III, who is a leading voice in the underground bizarro literature movement. Talk about a match made in a latex-bound razor-wired heaven.

There are, of course many other illustrations in this book that reflect Mr. Mironiuk's delightfully twisted and gloriously dark perspective. Disturbing? Most definitely. Beautiful? Without a doubt. Enjoy.

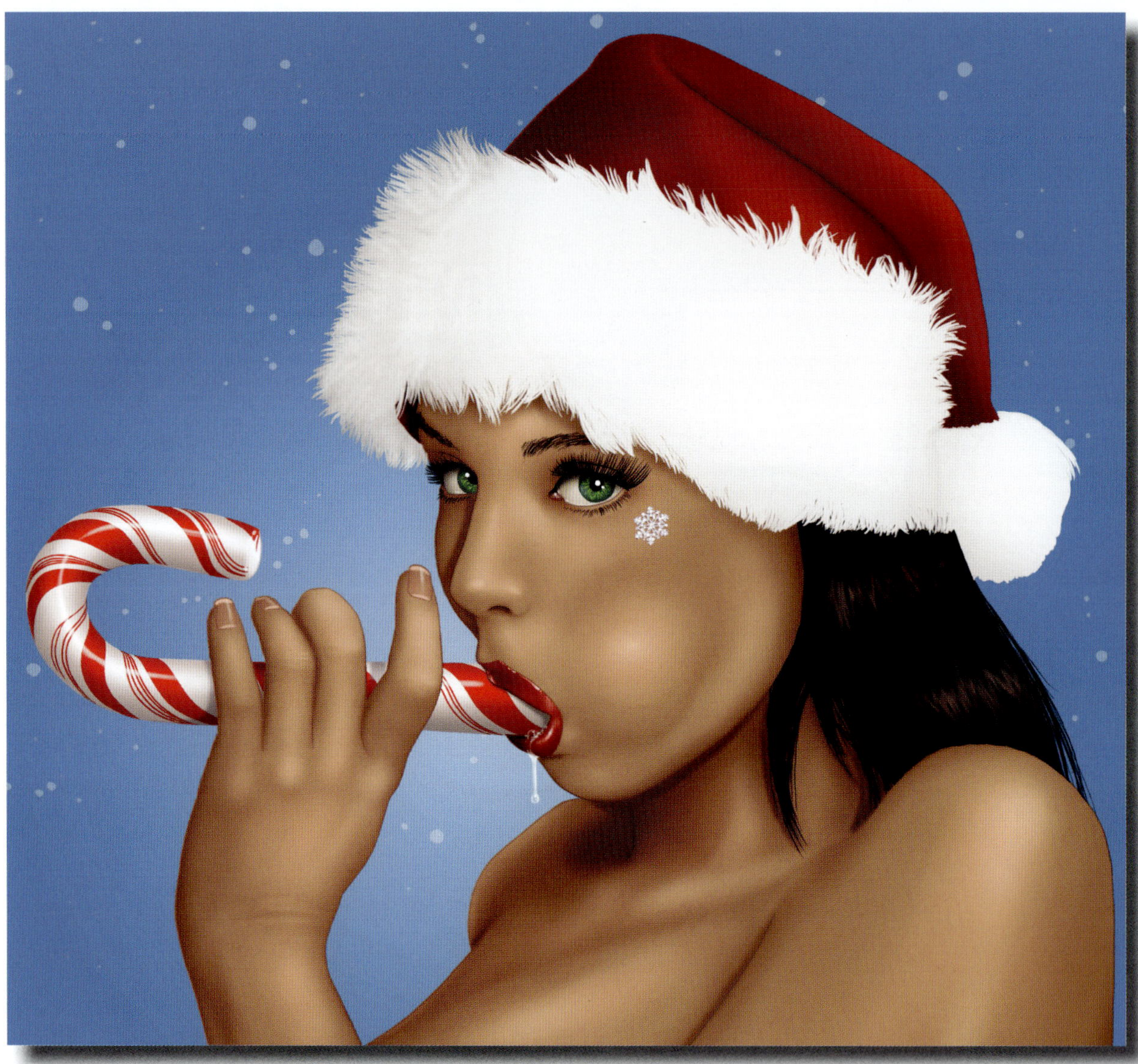

Ed Mironiuk is the love child of Rosemary Woodhouse. I'd put him very high on my list of heroes. Who else? Harry Earles, Valentia Cortese, Percy Helton, Clovis Trouille, Maria Falconetti, Krystof Komeda, Barbara Nichols, Louis Guglielmi, Jack E. Leonard – all people doing their thing, if you like, but not just doing it: doing it with an instinctive sense of shape and form, and bringing it off without visible effort. What Kenneth Tynan called 'high definition performance'. His paintings display extreme innocence and considerable danger, like something hanging in a secret vault on the Good Ship Lollipop.

STEPHEN SAYADIAN/
Rinse Dream

For the latest Mironiuk creations, both cute and kinky go to www.edmironiuk.com

Disturbing Beauty
The Bizarro Art of Ed Mironiuk

Book design by Grassy Knoll Studios.

Published by SQP Inc.
PO Box 248 - Columbus NJ 08022

Sal Quartuccio & Bob Keenan - Publishers

For a free, full color catalog showcasing the entire SQP line of erotic, fantasy, and pin-up artwork, go to:
www.sqpartbooks.com

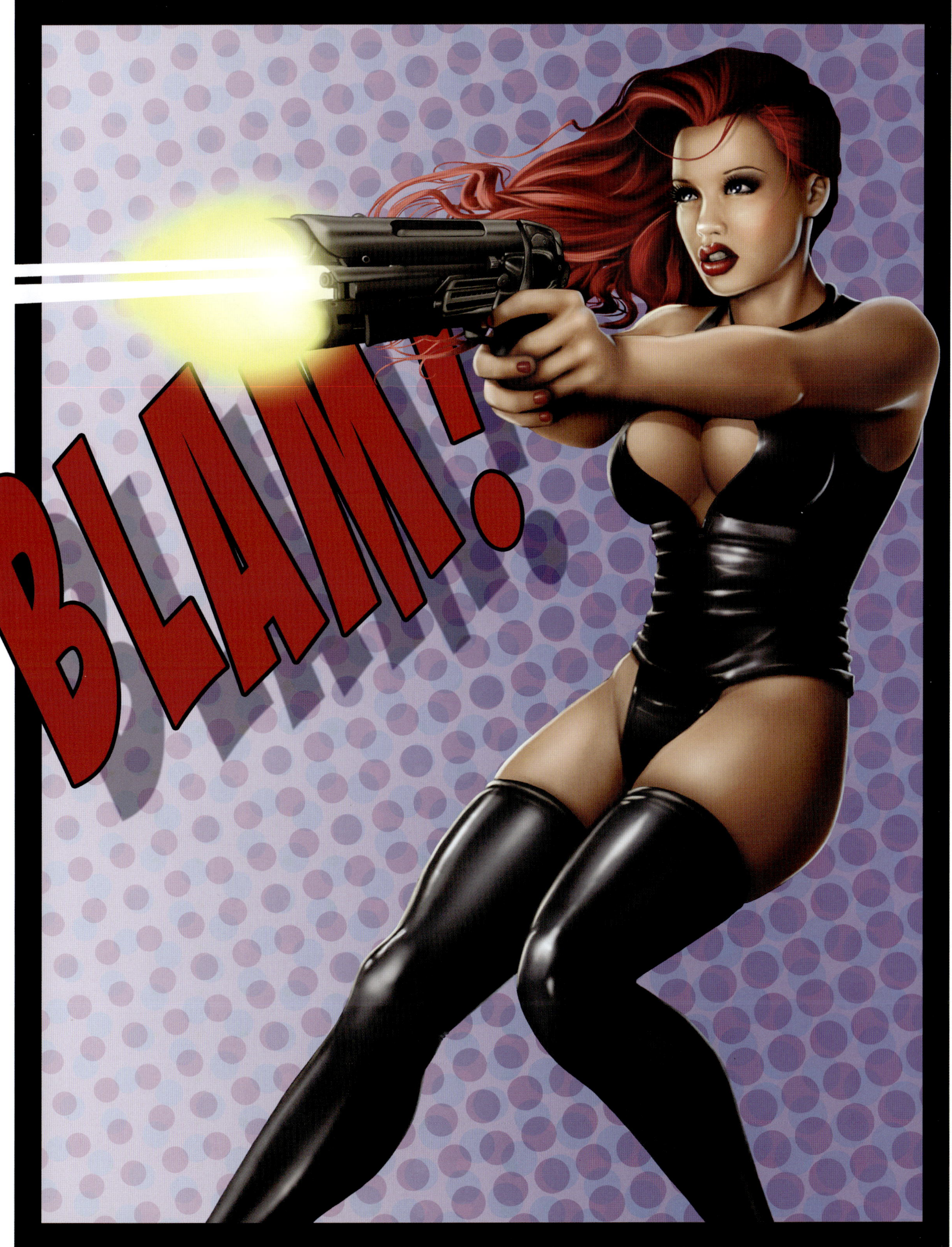

Assassin

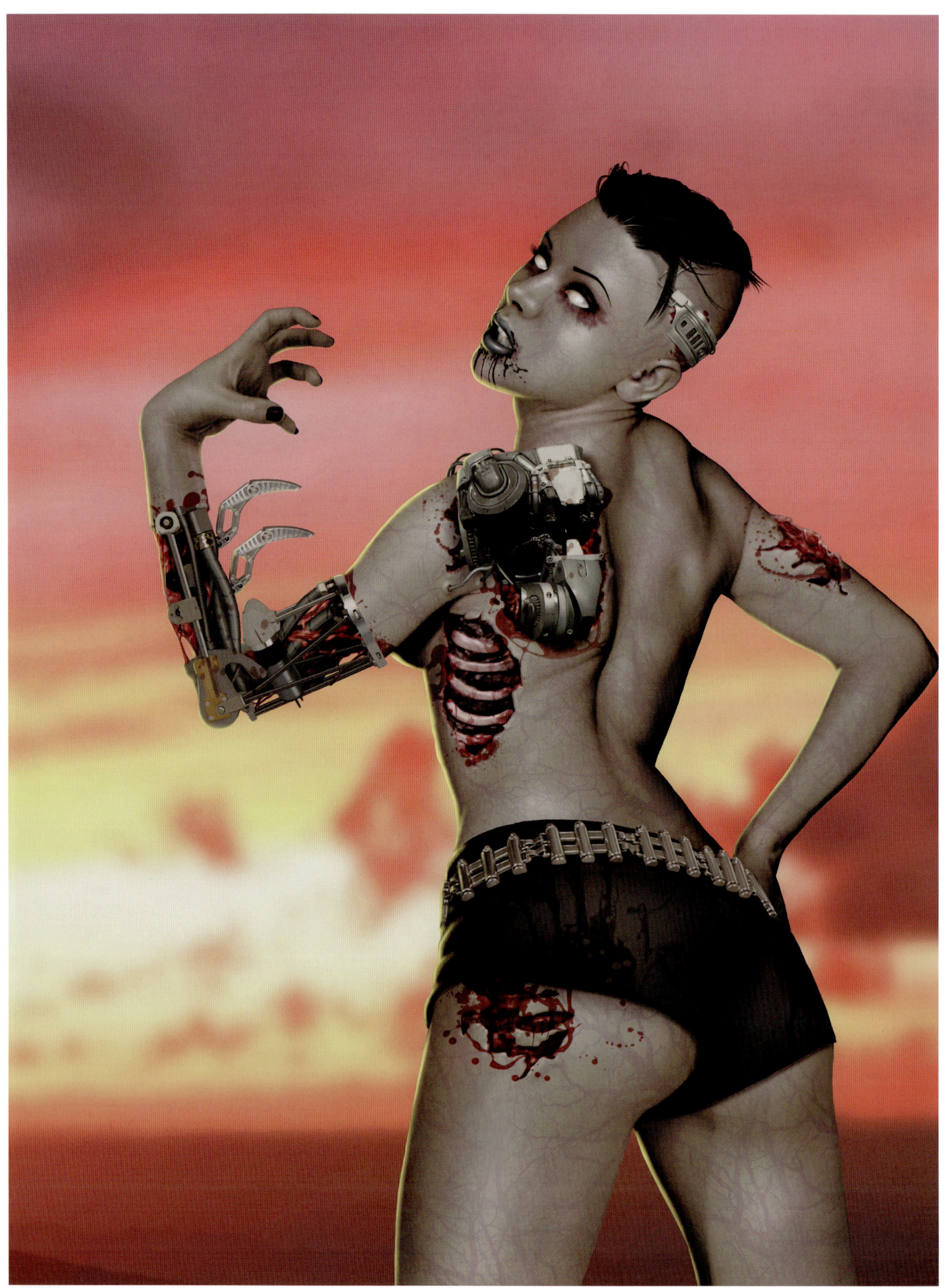

Electric Jesus Corpse

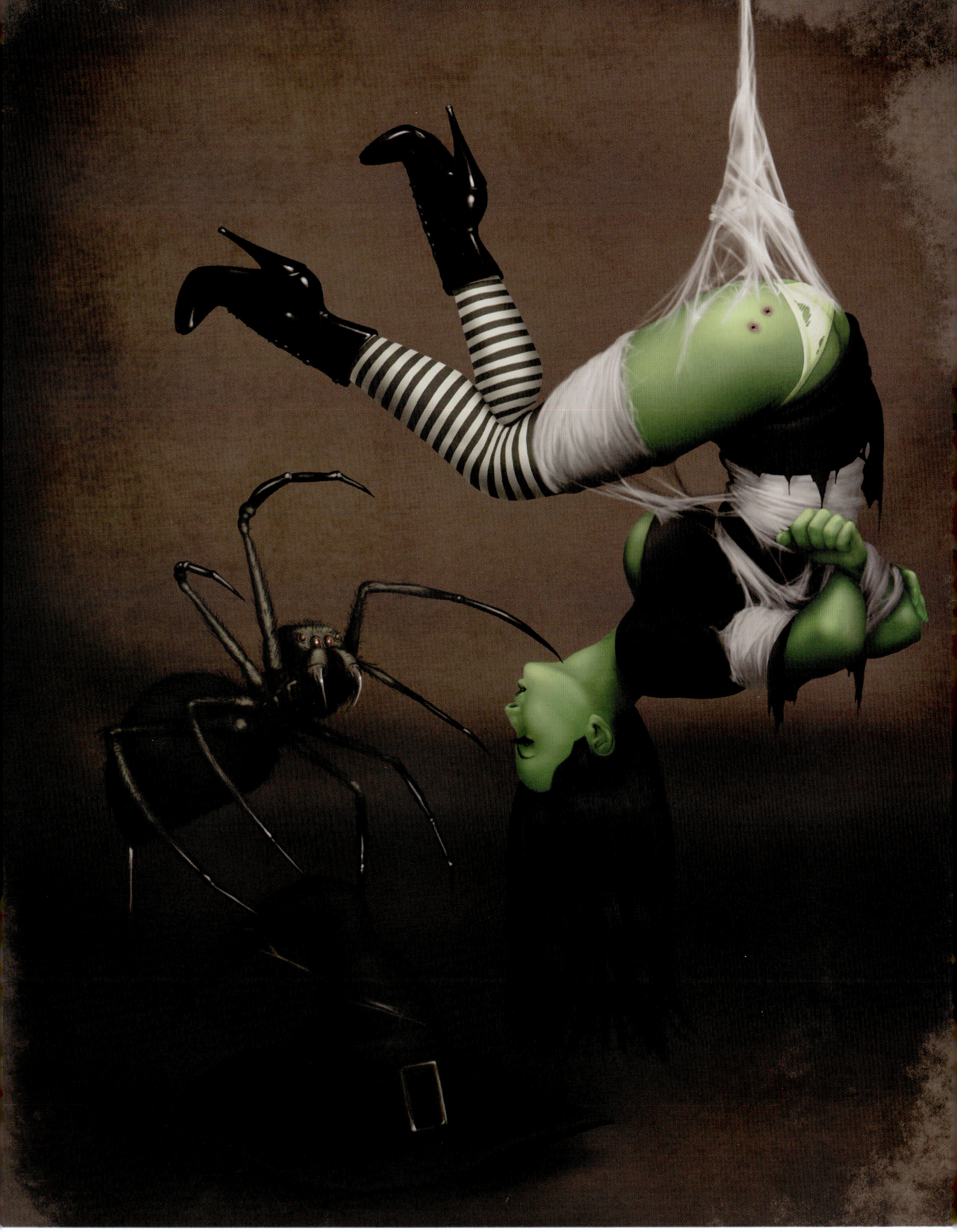

Shabari Witch

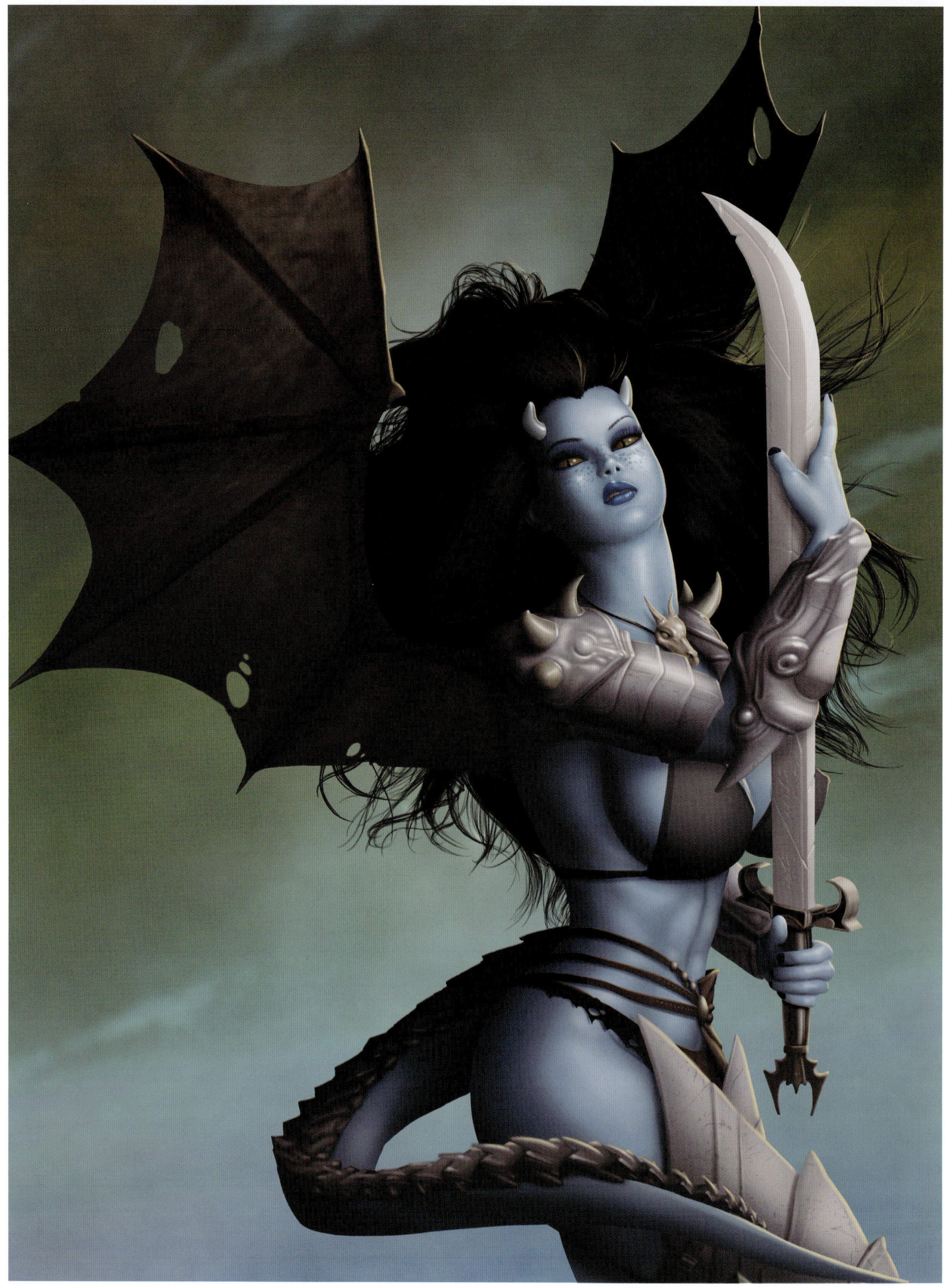

Dragon Slayer

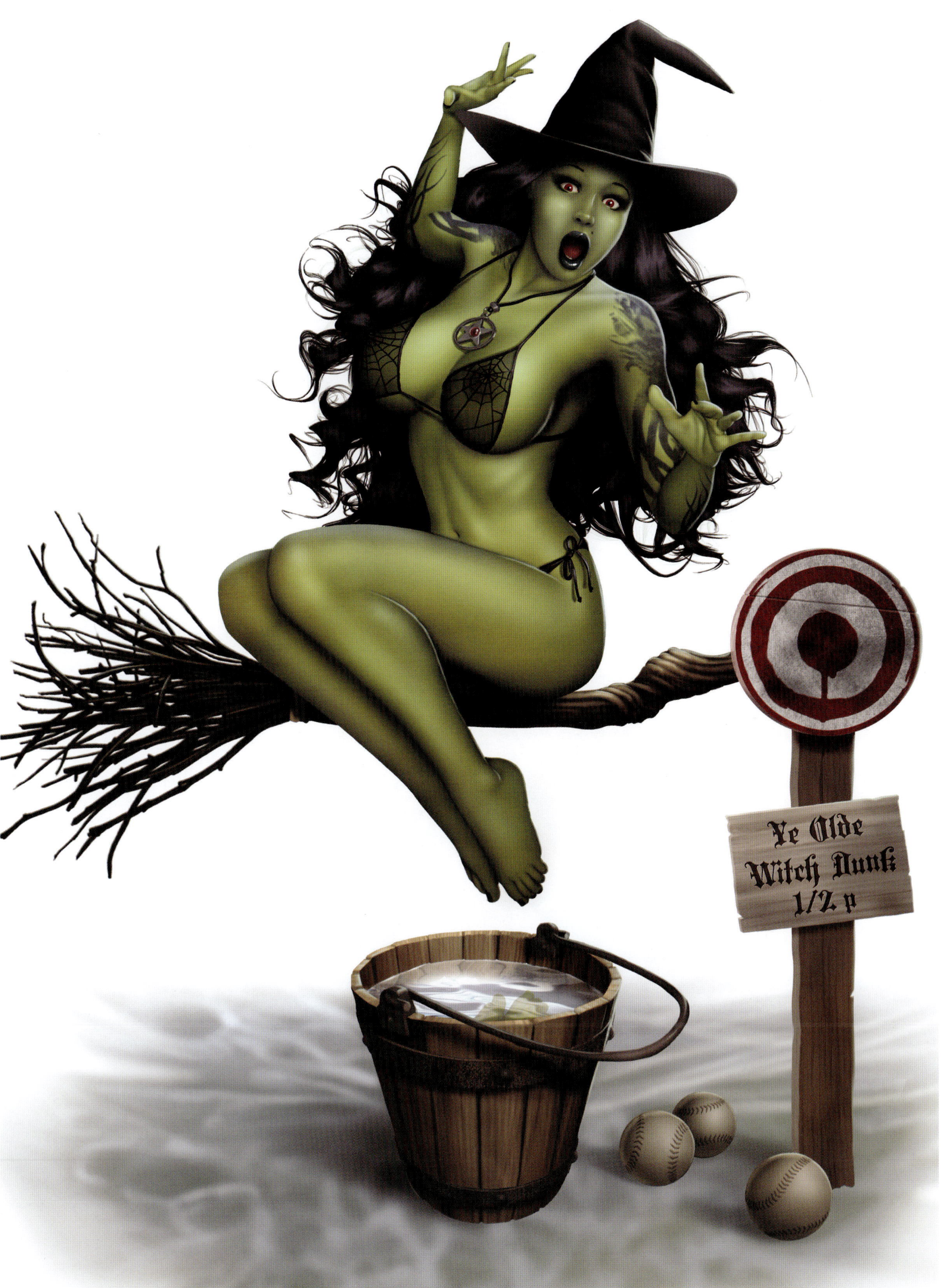

Witch Dunk

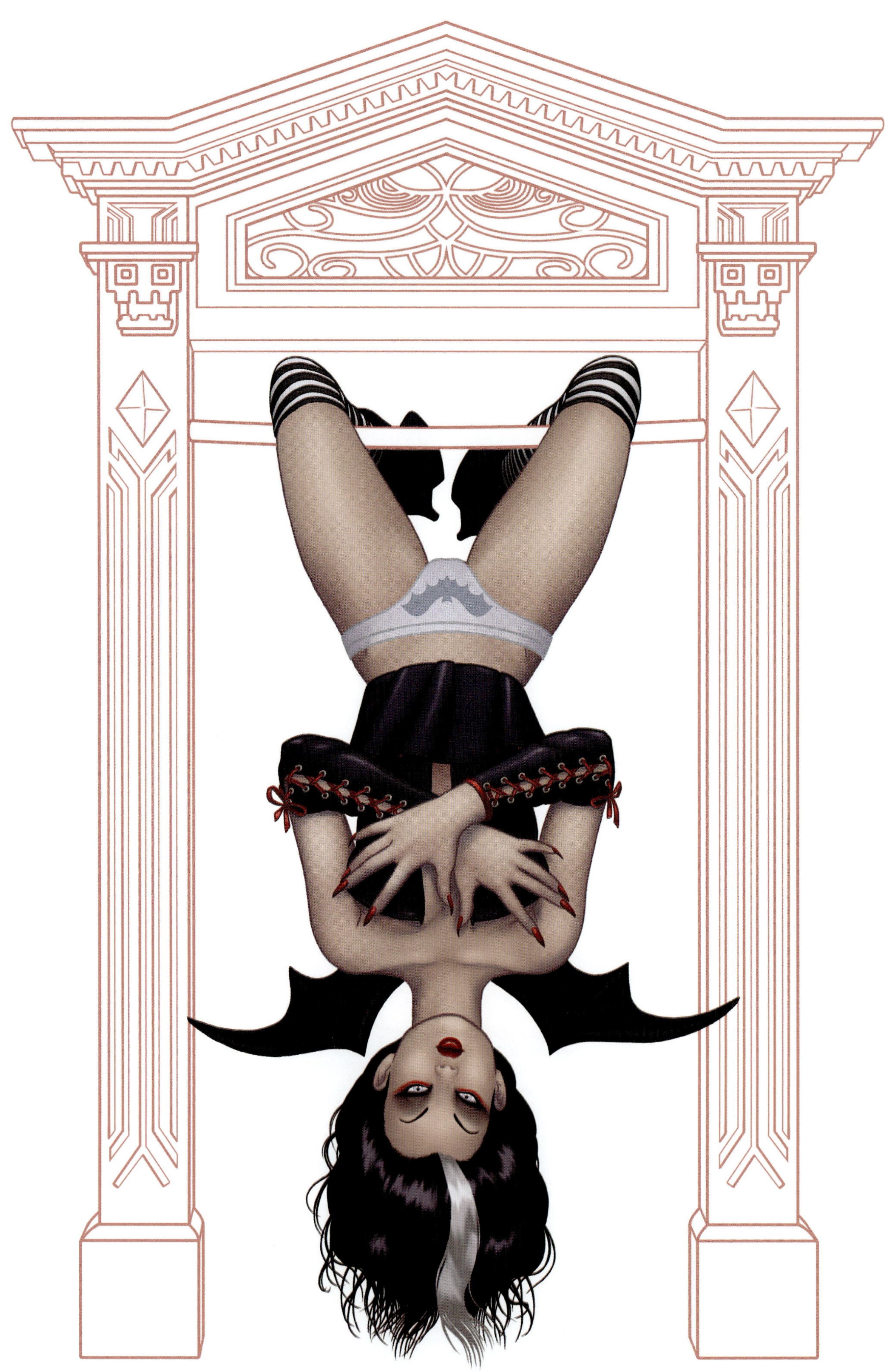

Corruptible

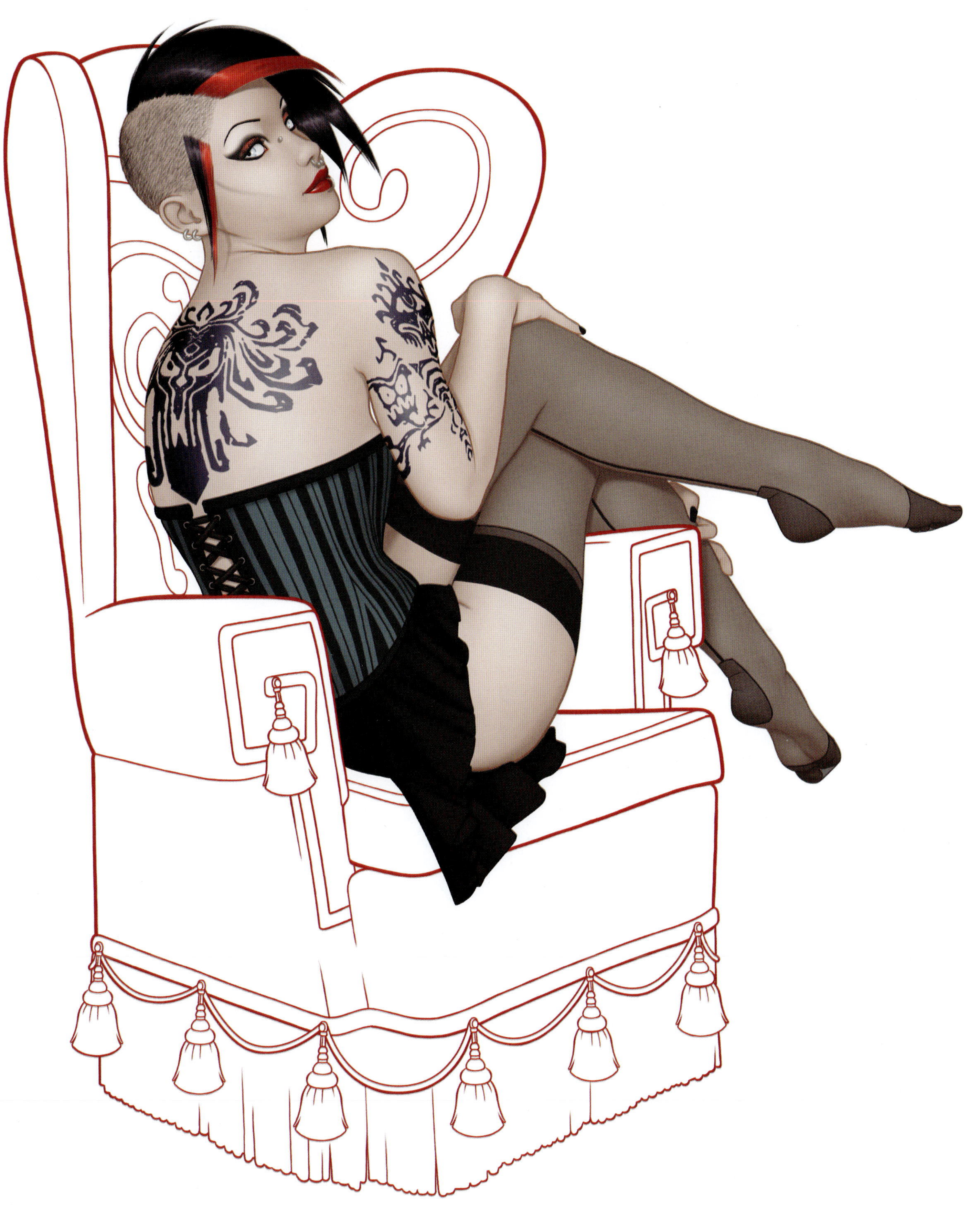

Bea Witch

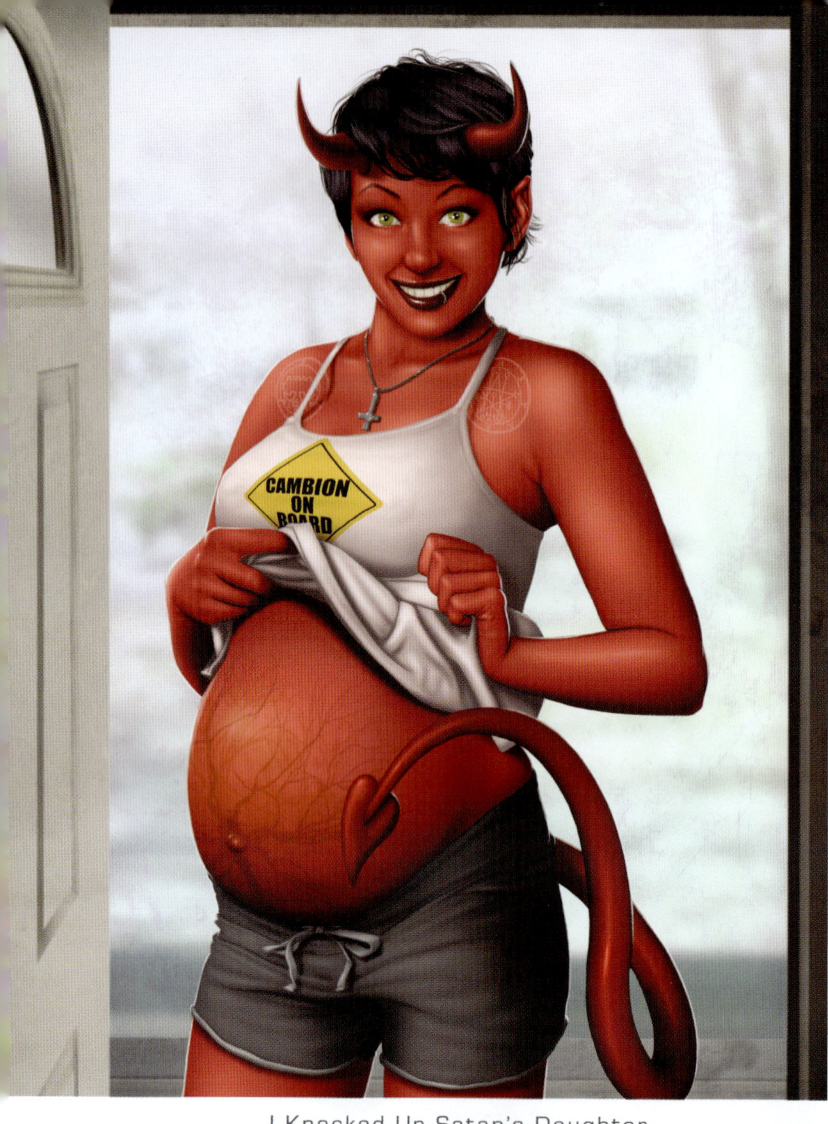

I Knocked Up Satan's Daughter

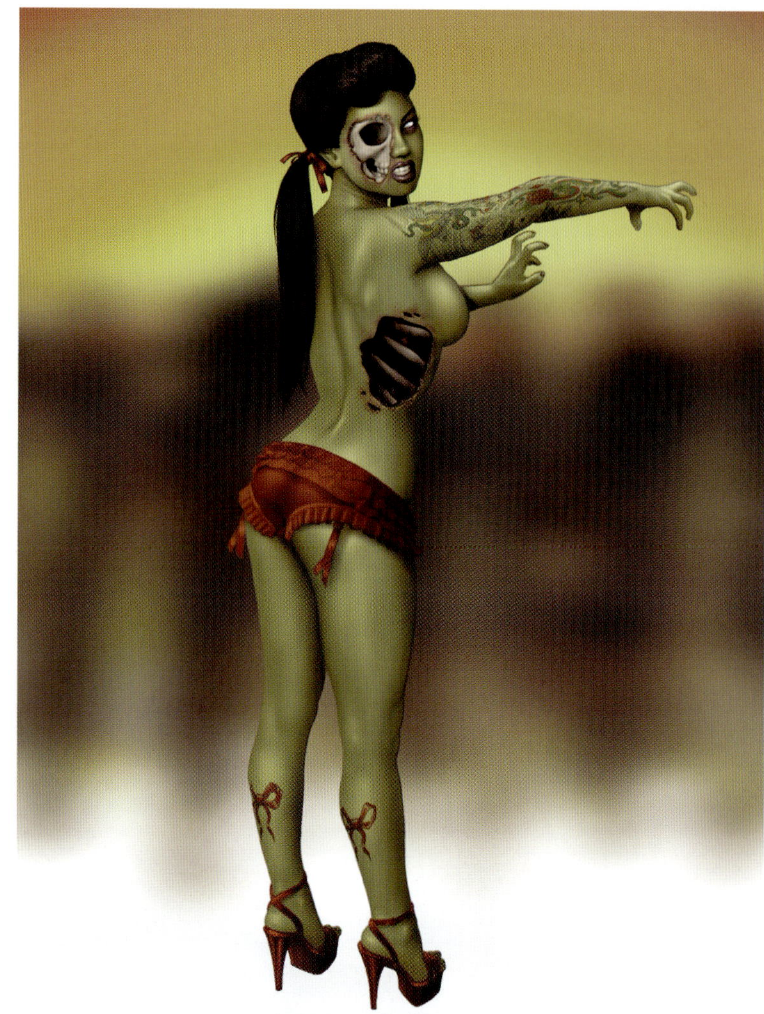

Donna The Dead

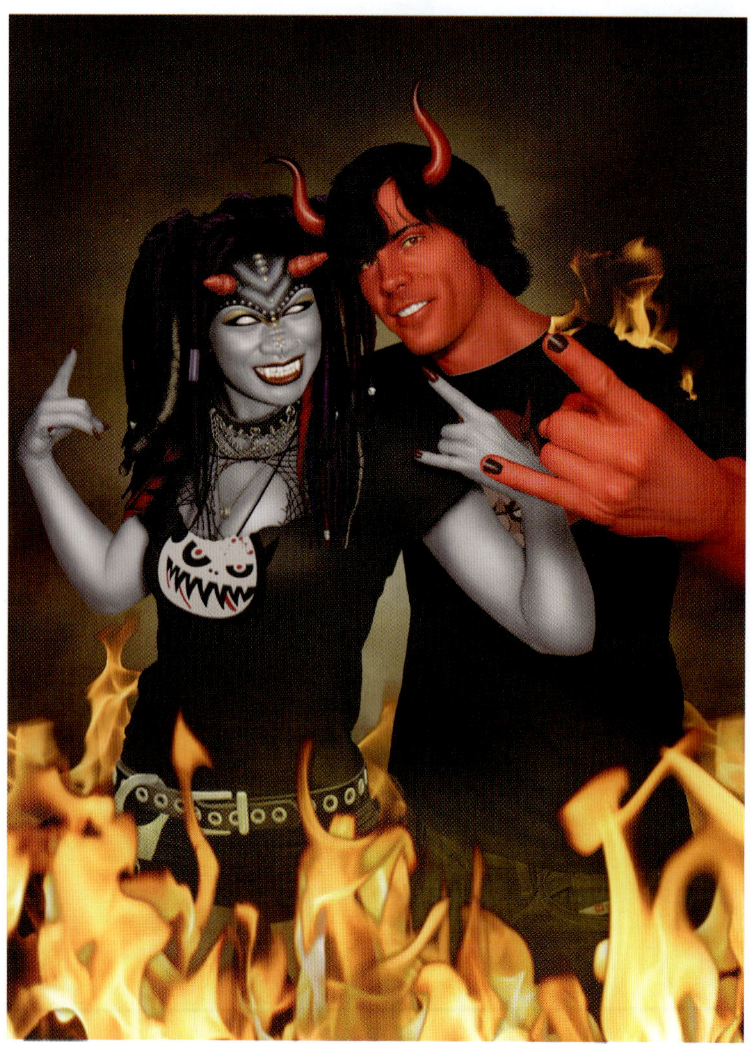

Demon Weekend

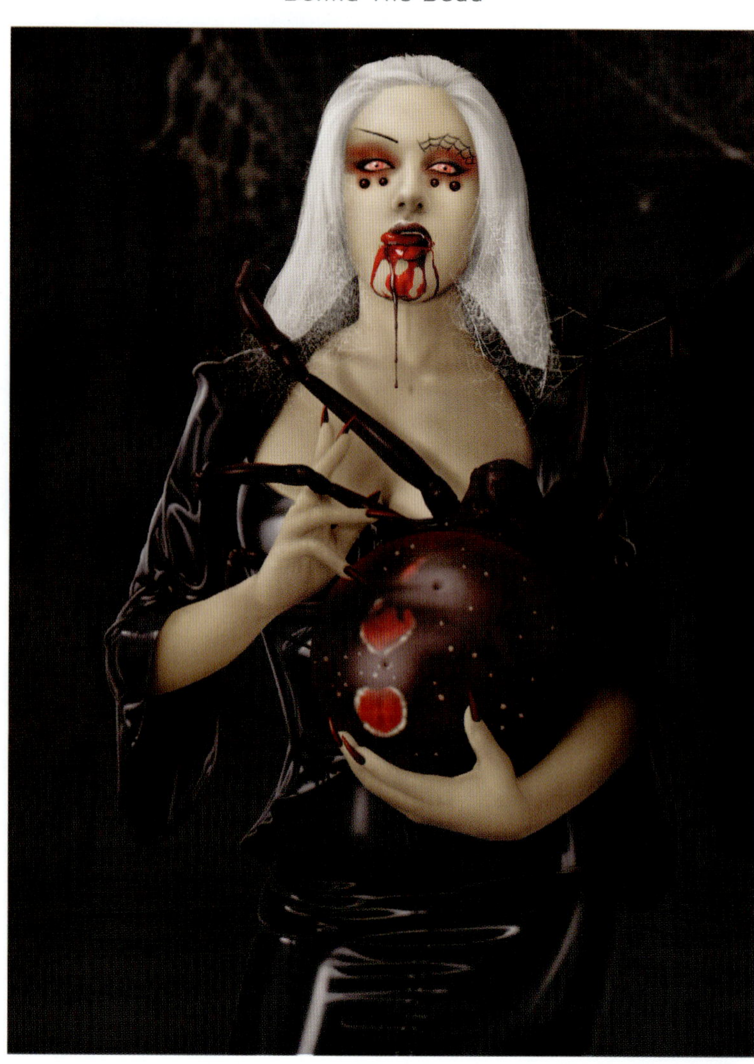

Spider

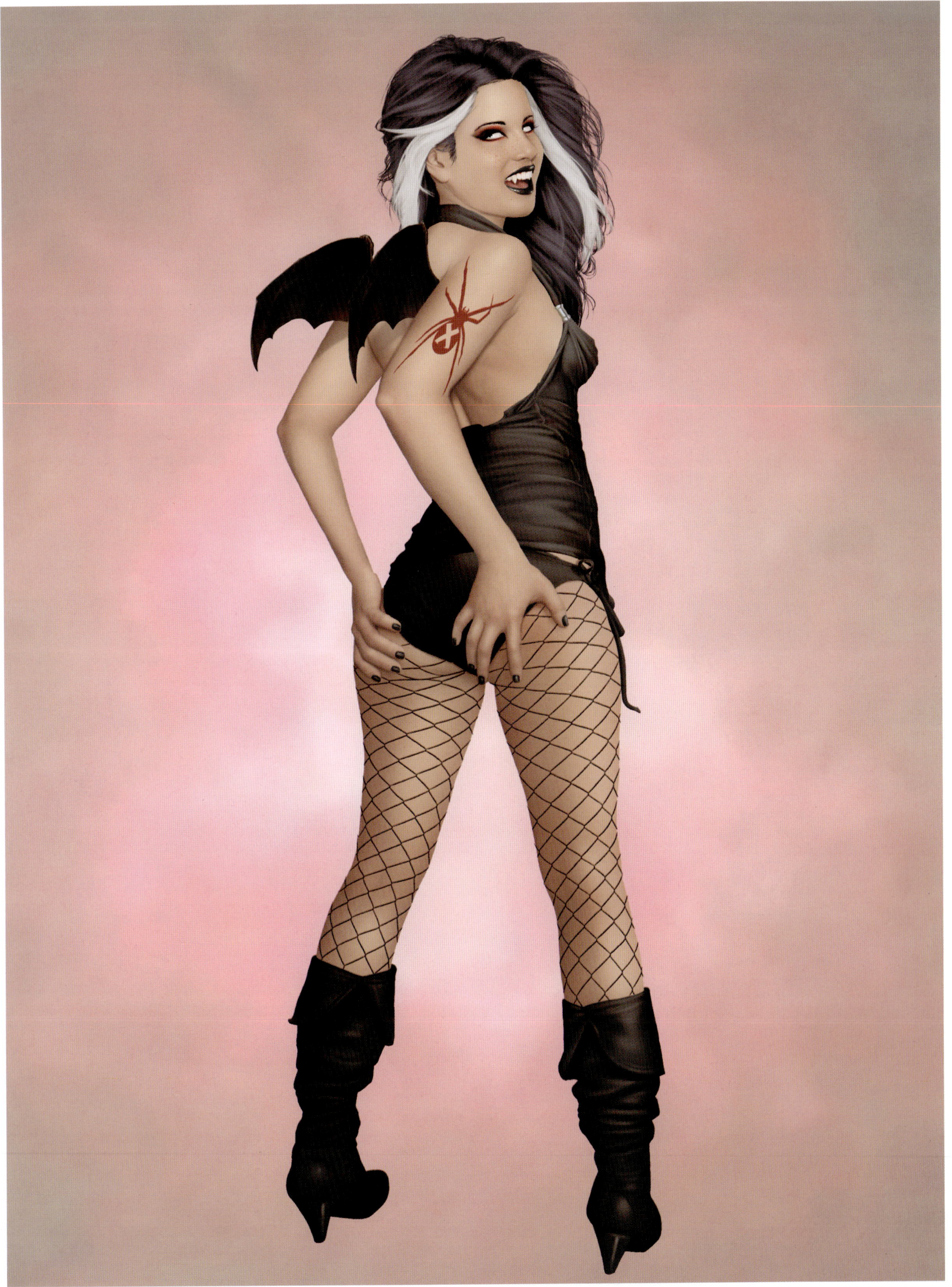

Vamp

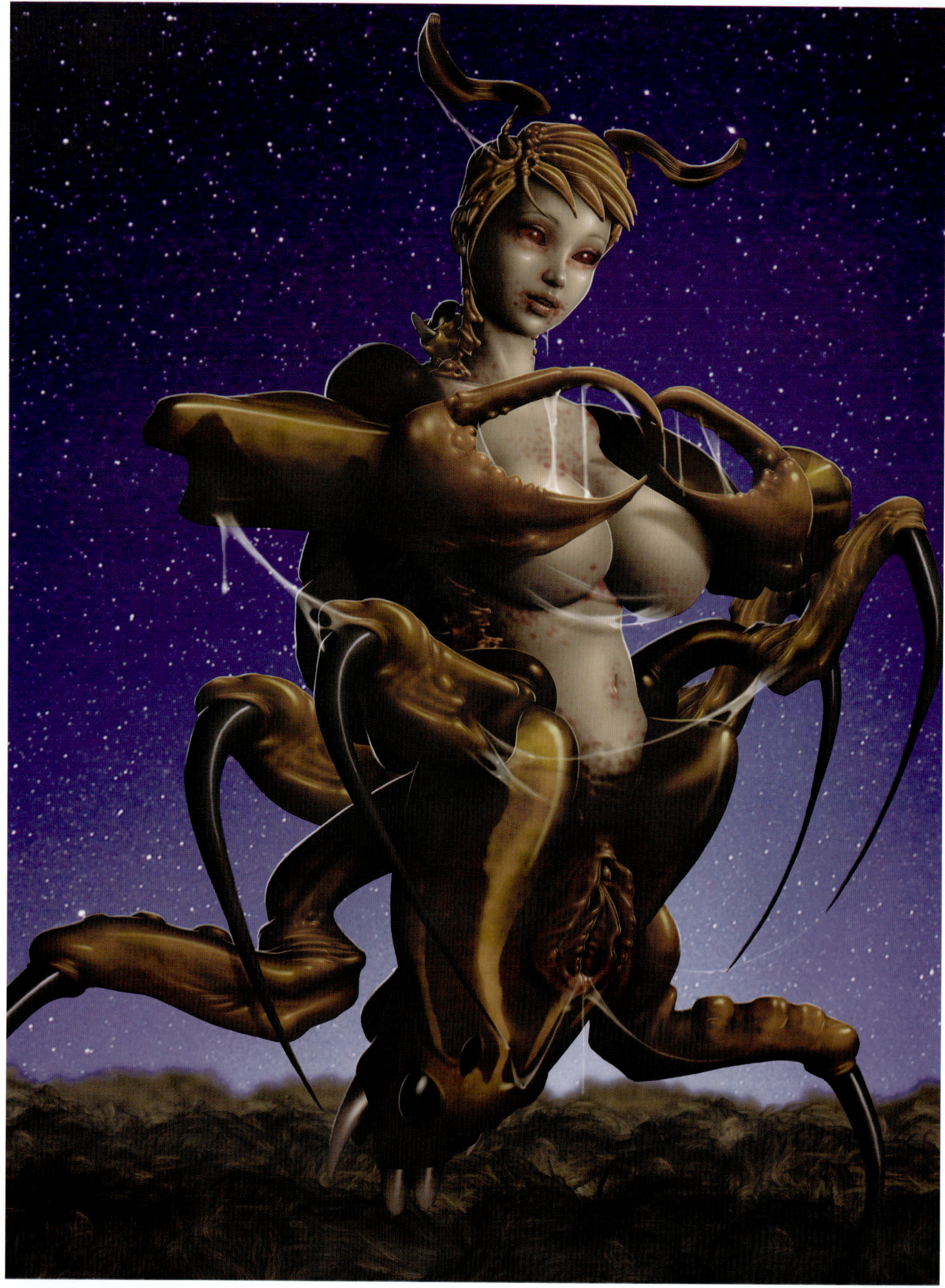

The Tick People

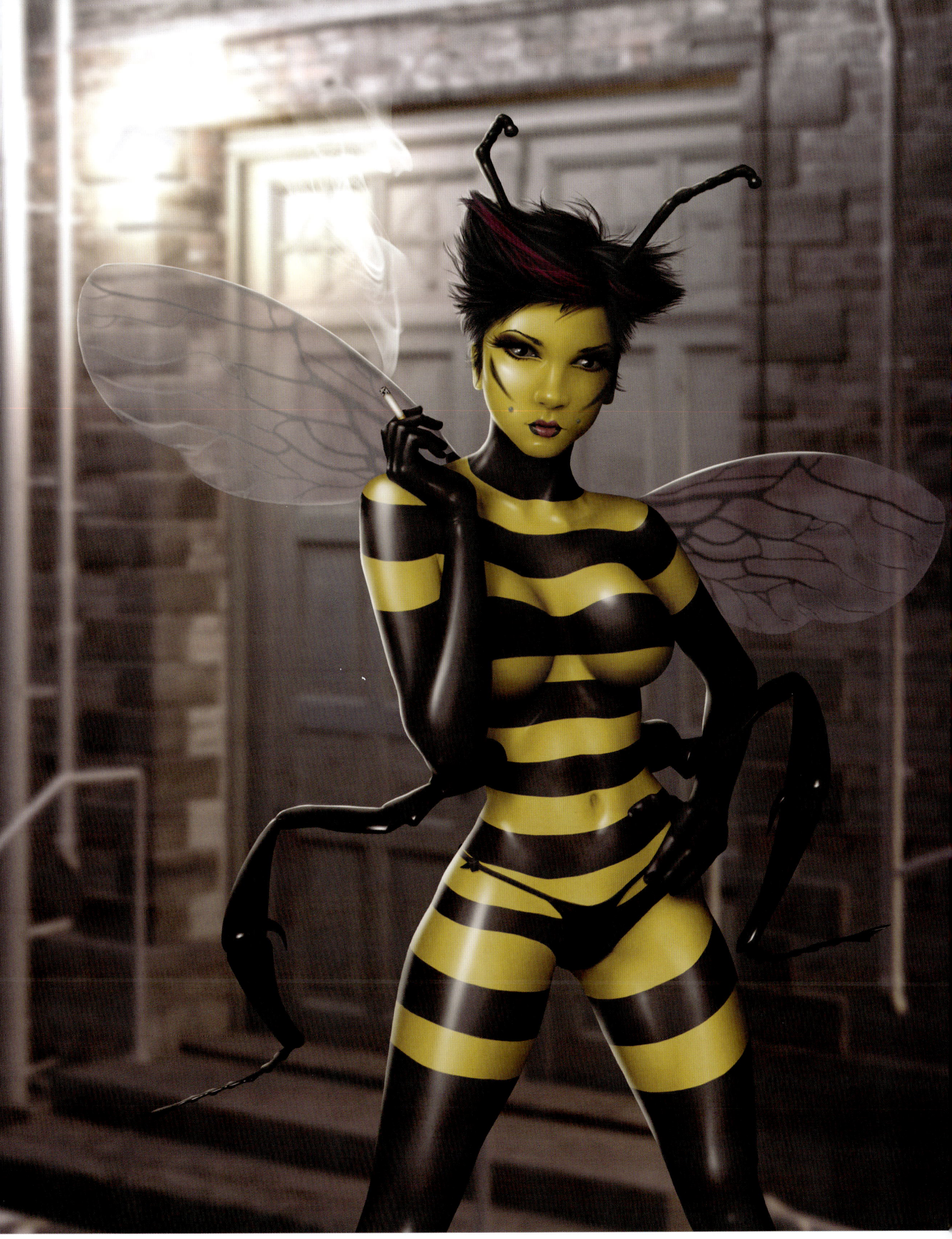

Hungry Bug

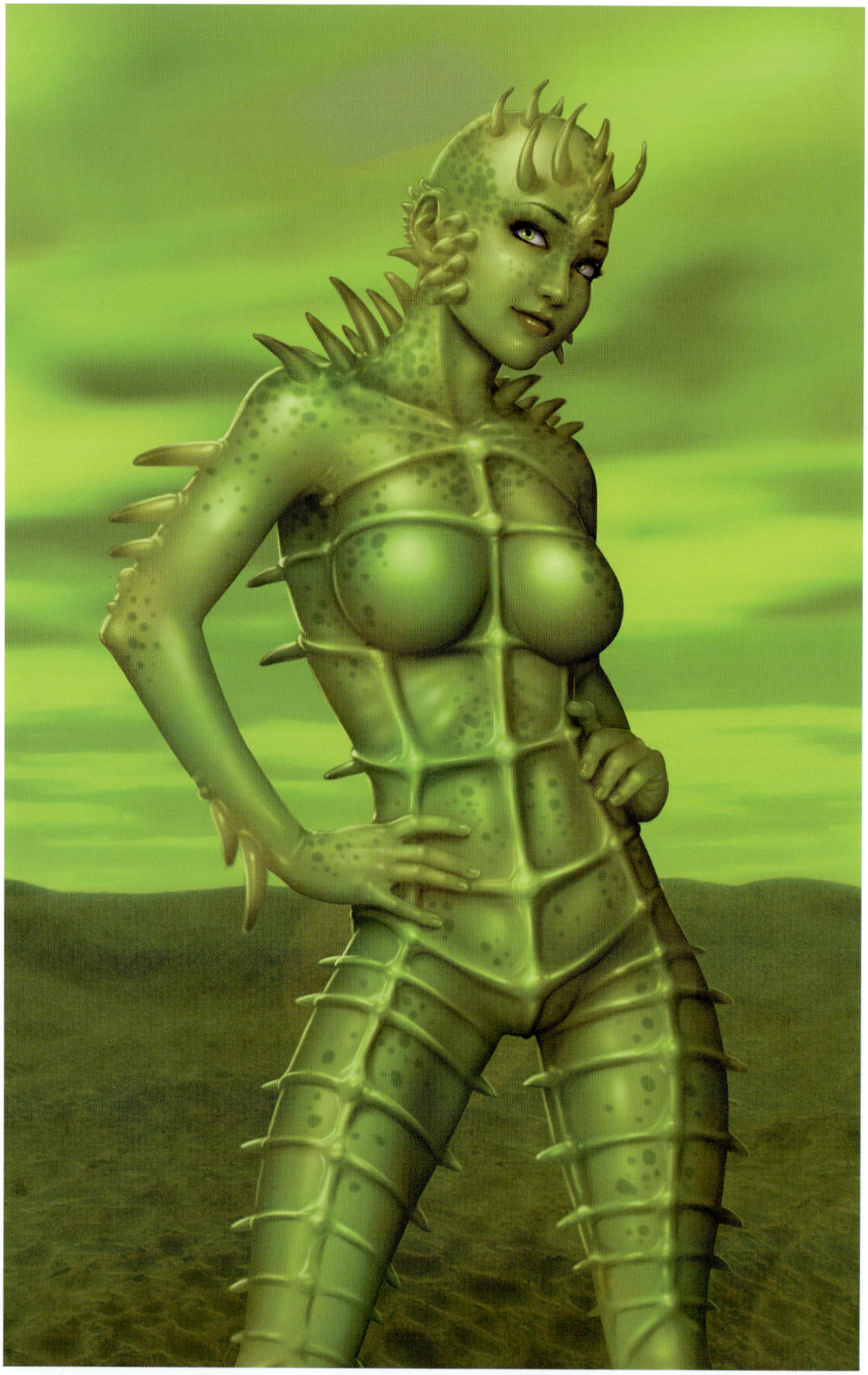

Ugly Heaven, Beautiful Hell

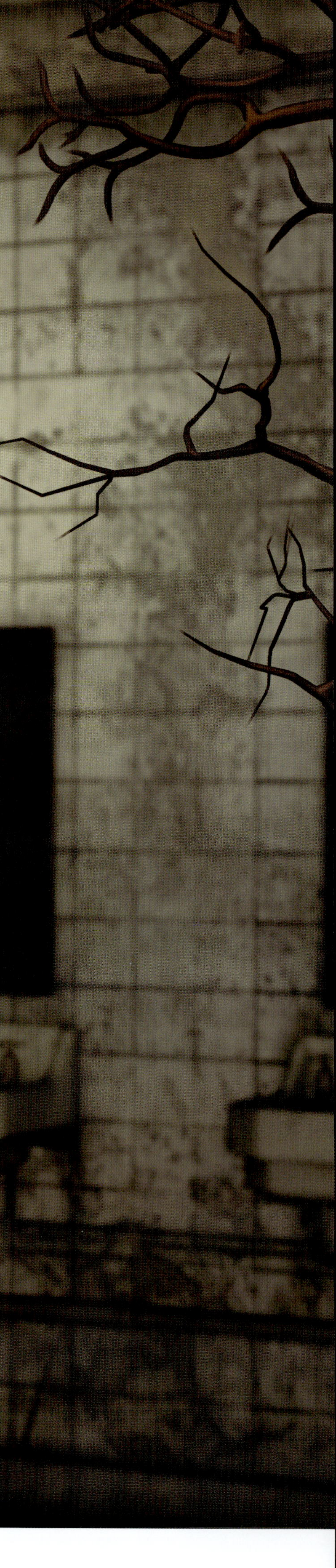

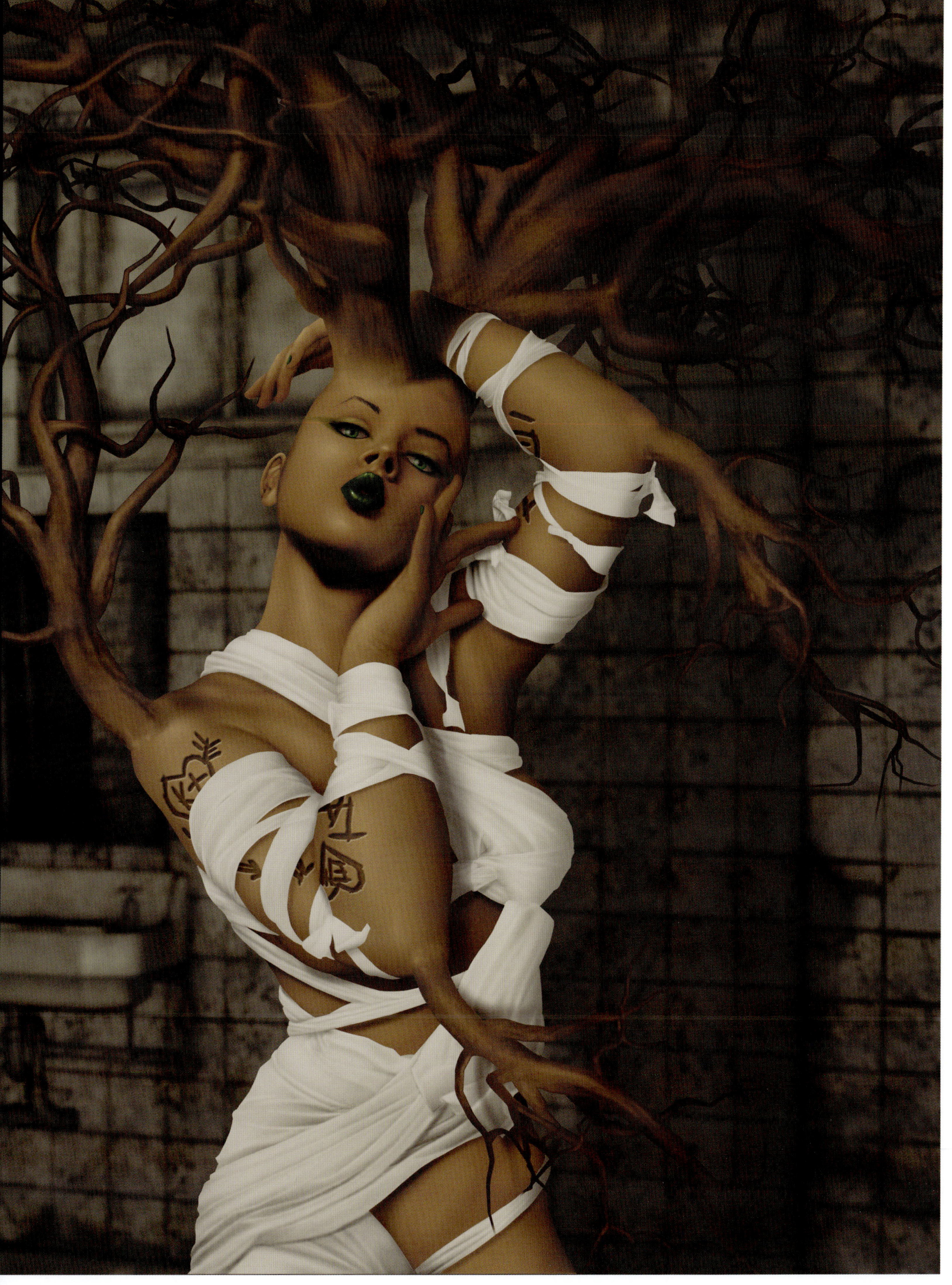

Seeking Oblivion

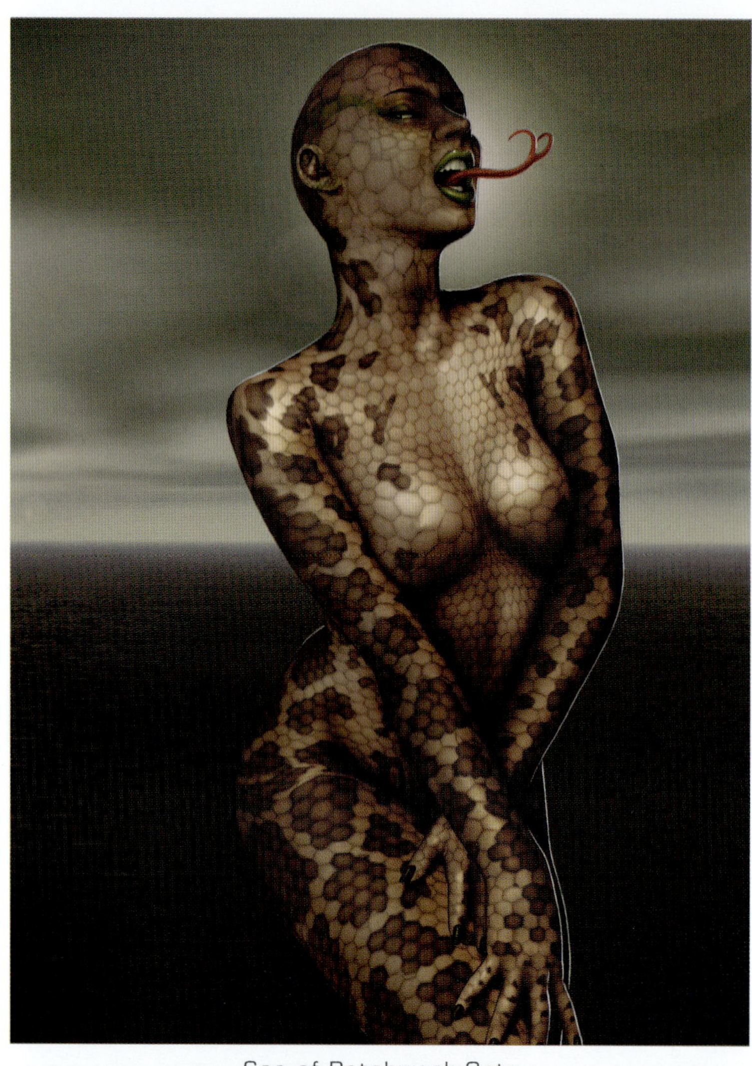

Sea of Patchwork Cats

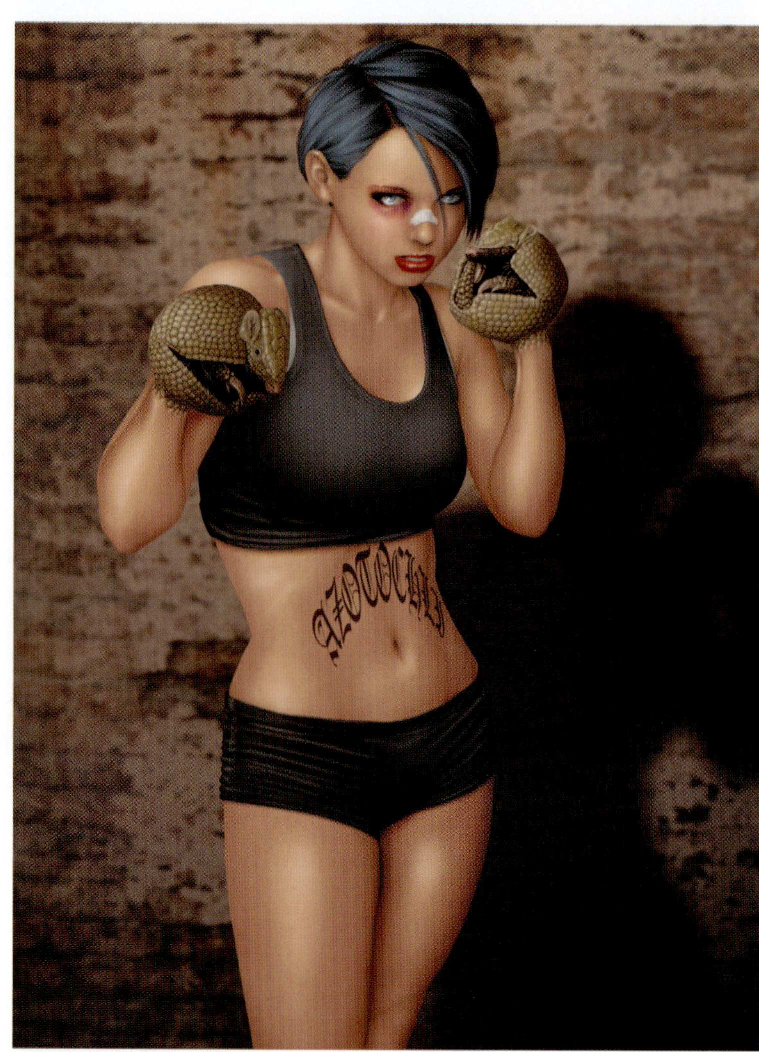

Armadillo Fists

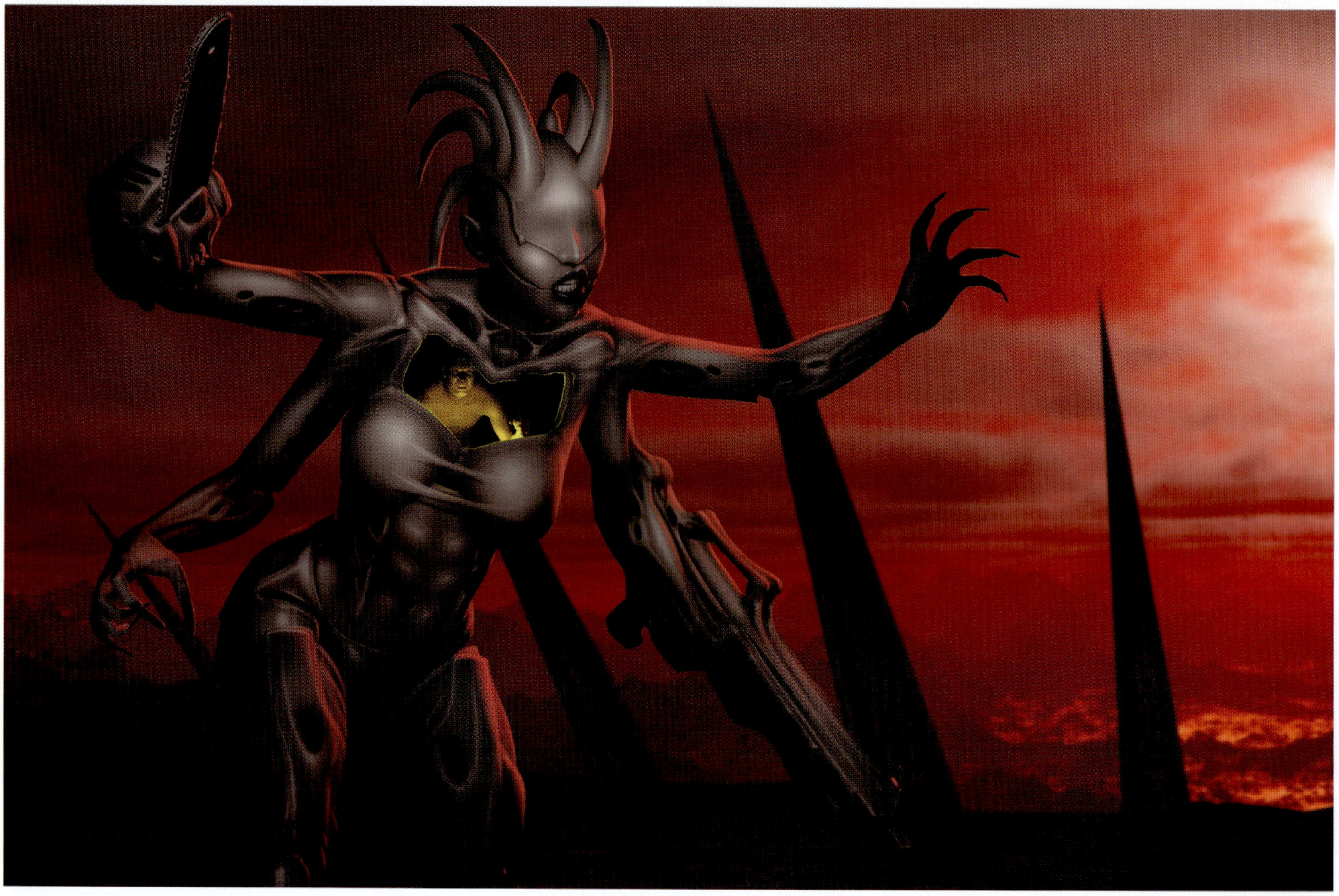

Chainsaw Heart

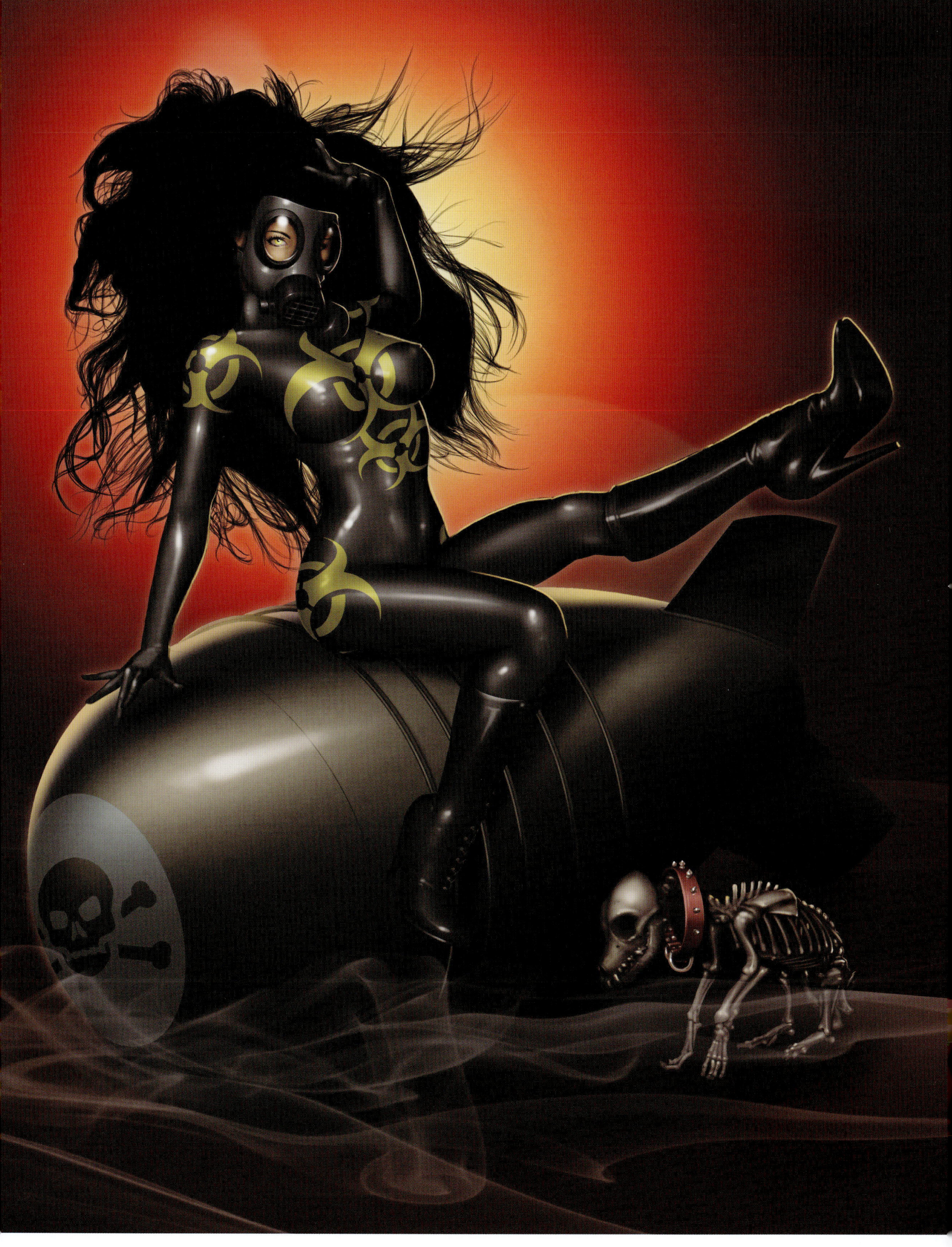

Crab Town

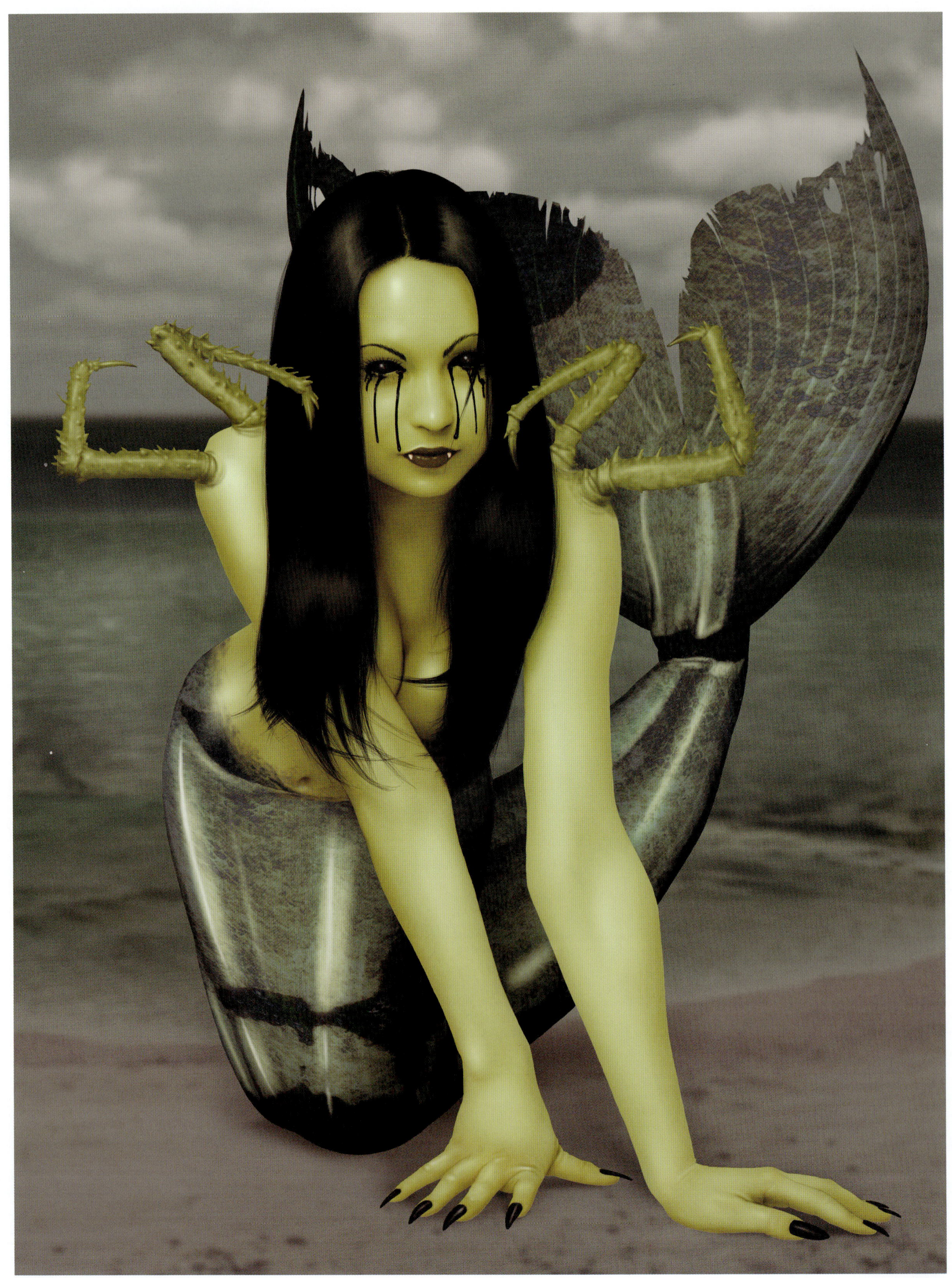

Village of Mermaids

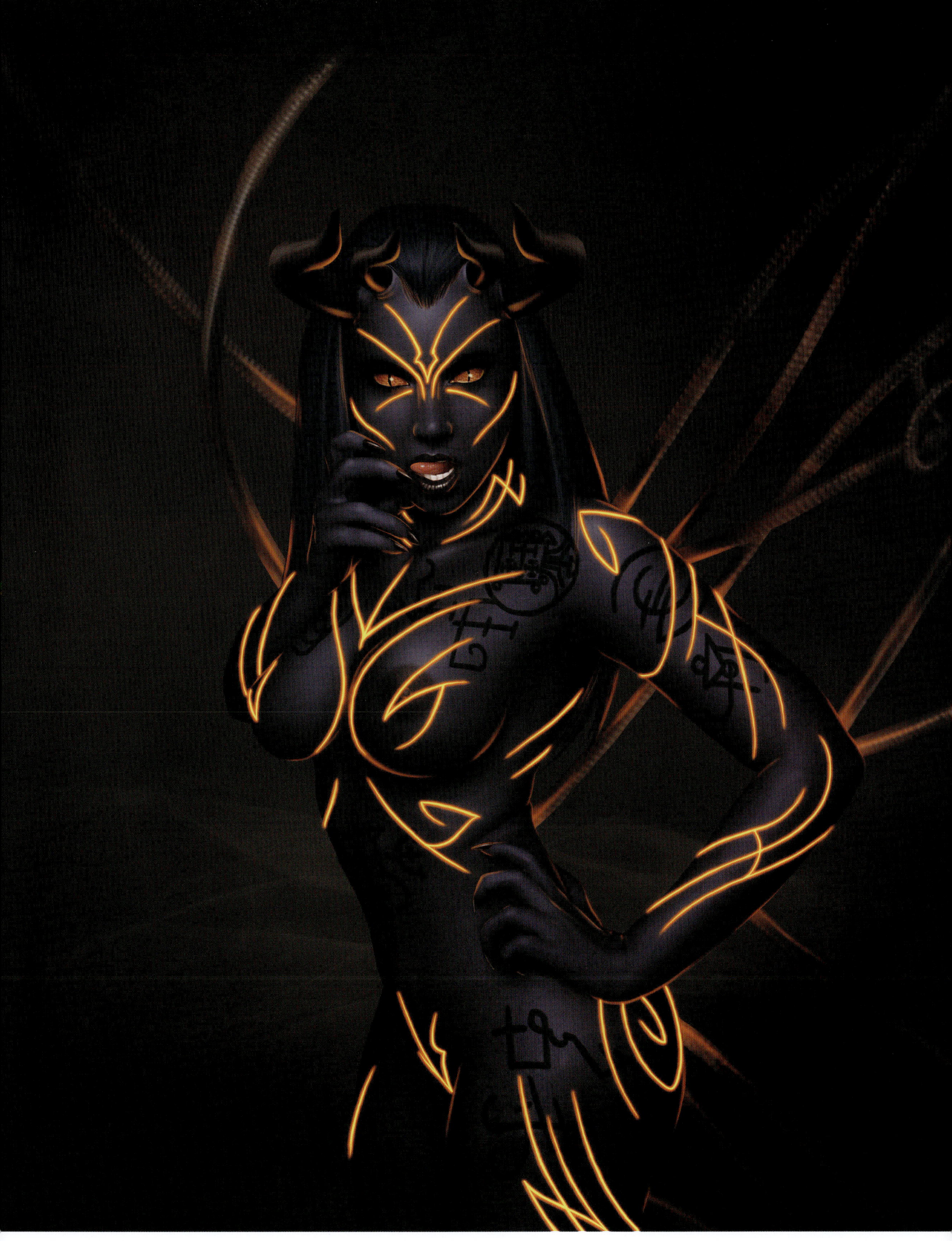

Cyber Demon

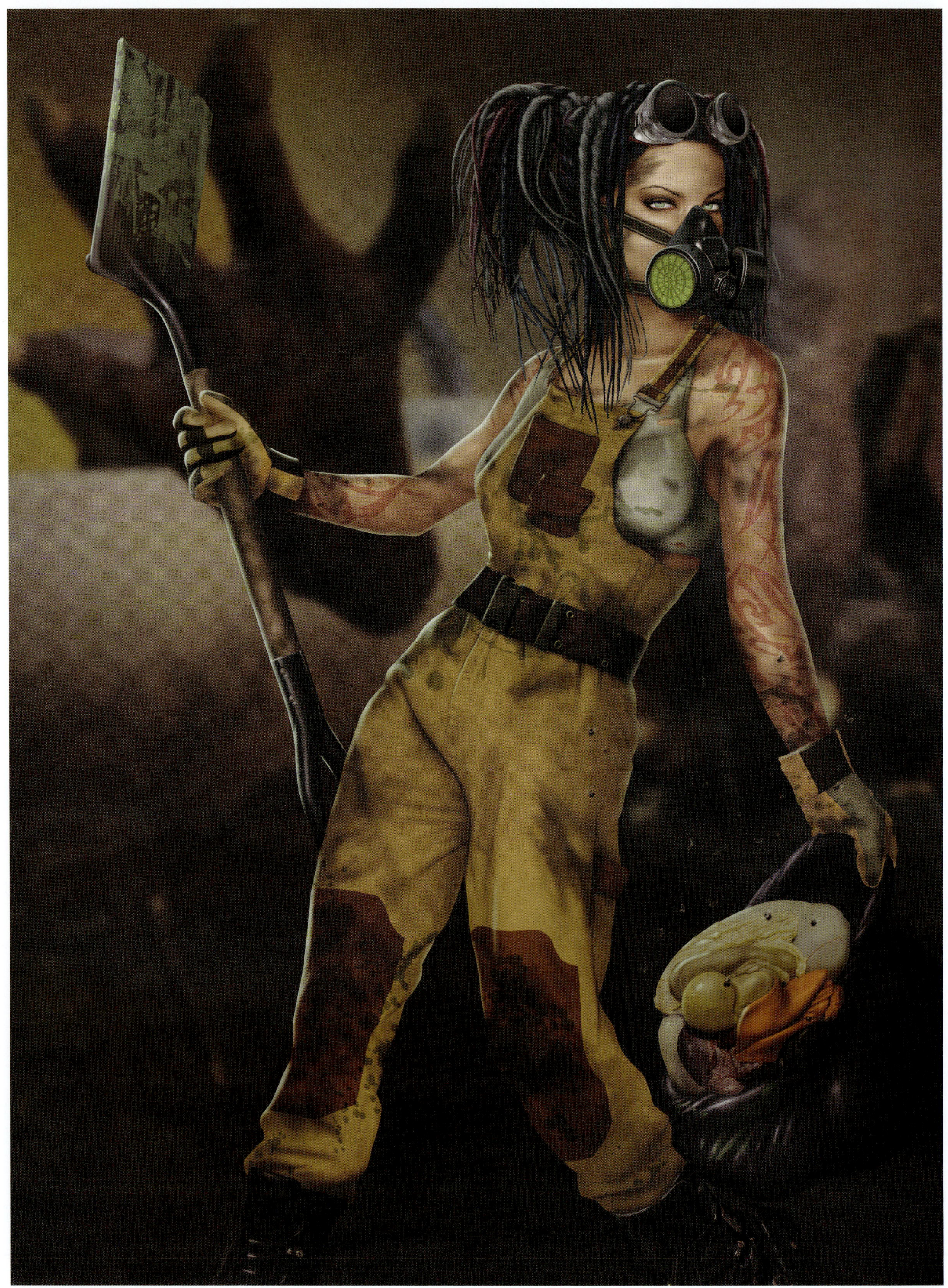

Clean Up Crew

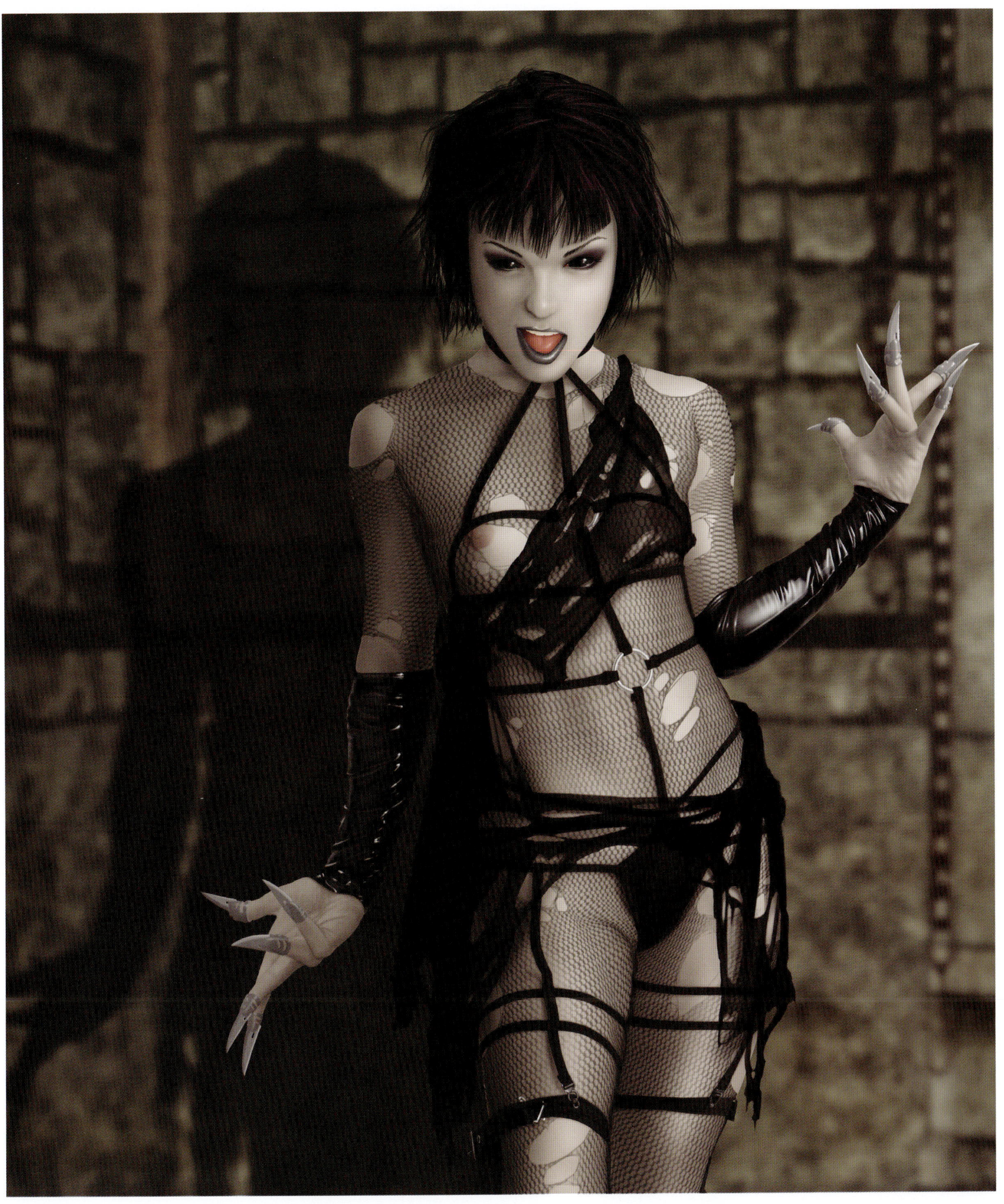

Razor Wire Pubic Hair

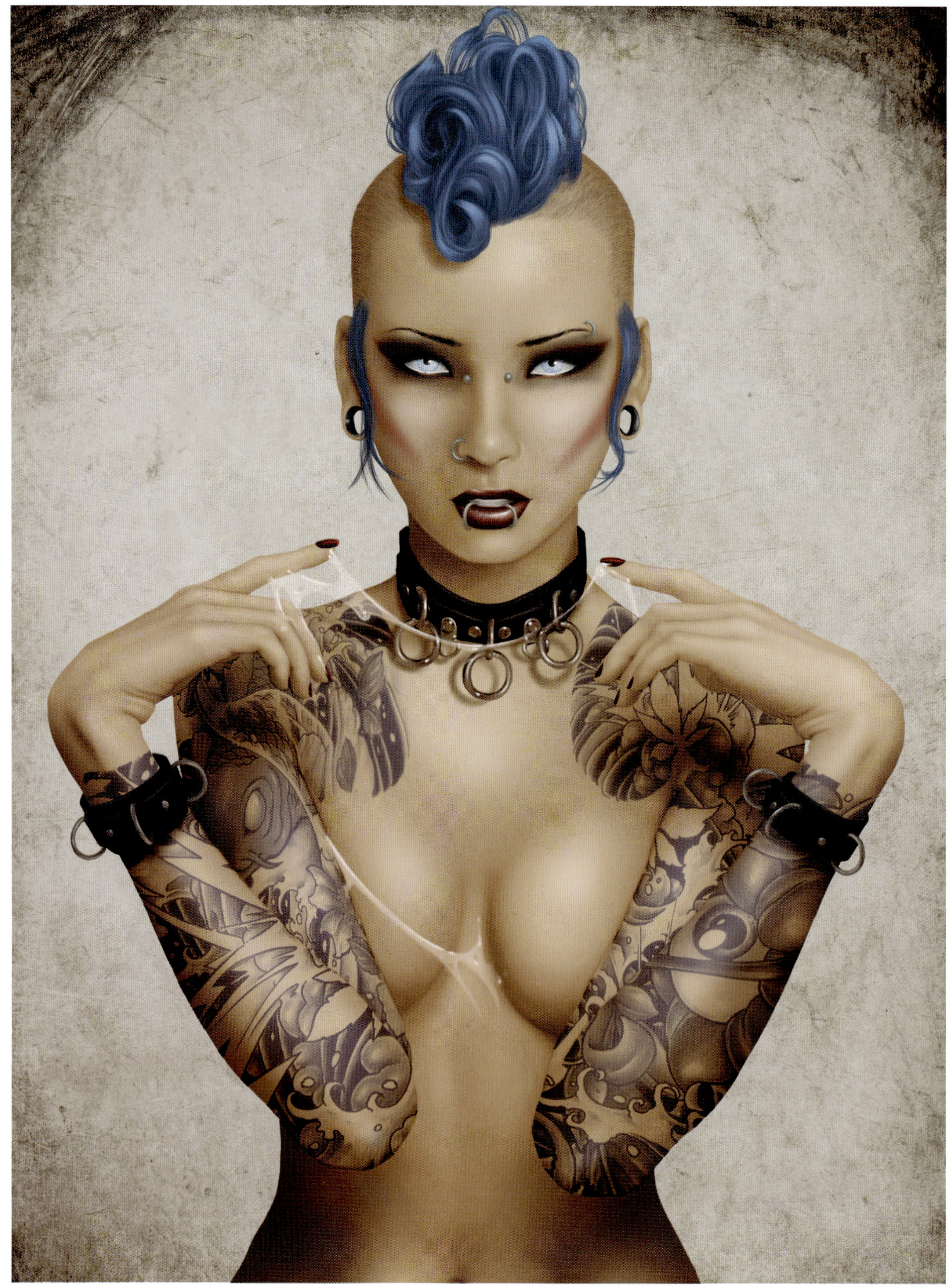

Full Metal Octopus

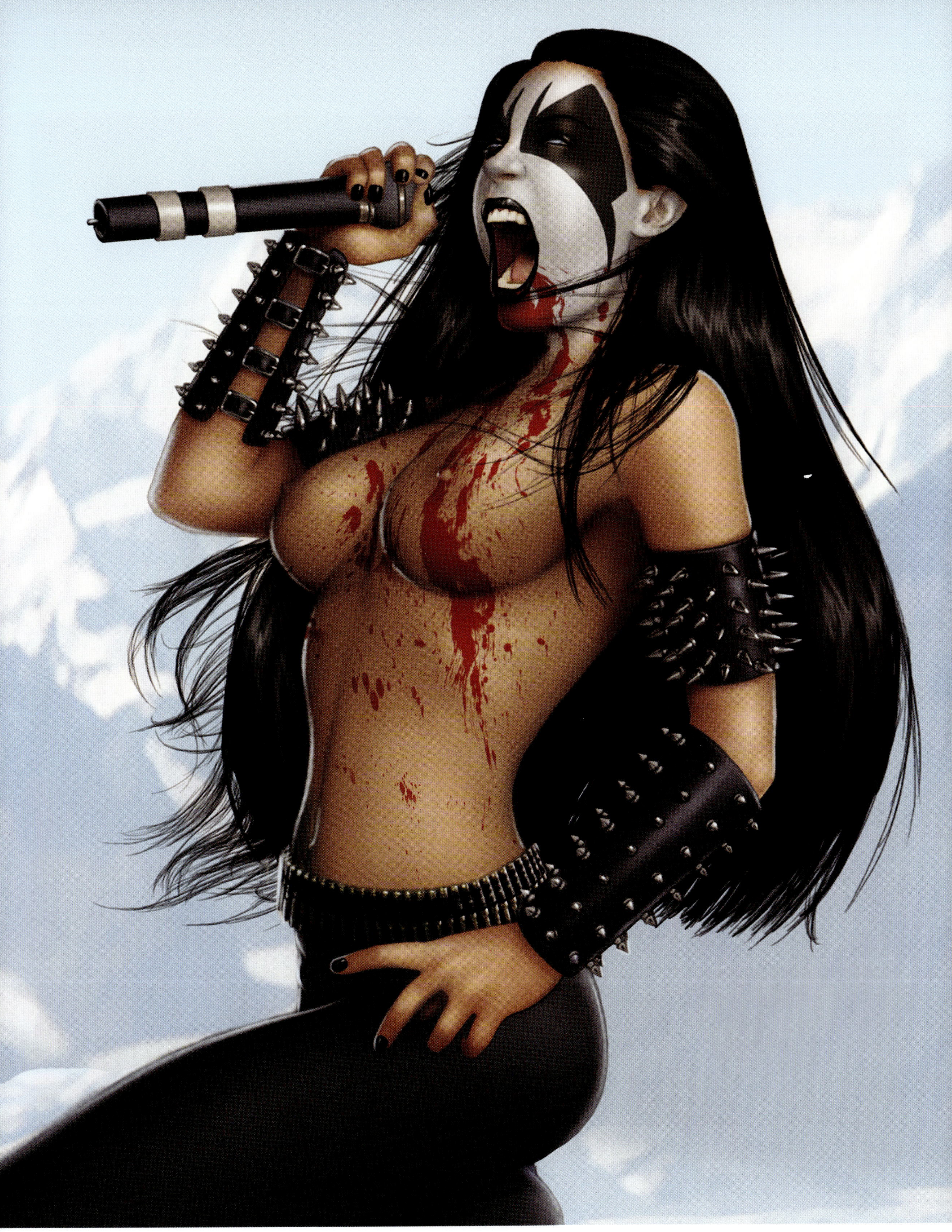

Black Metal

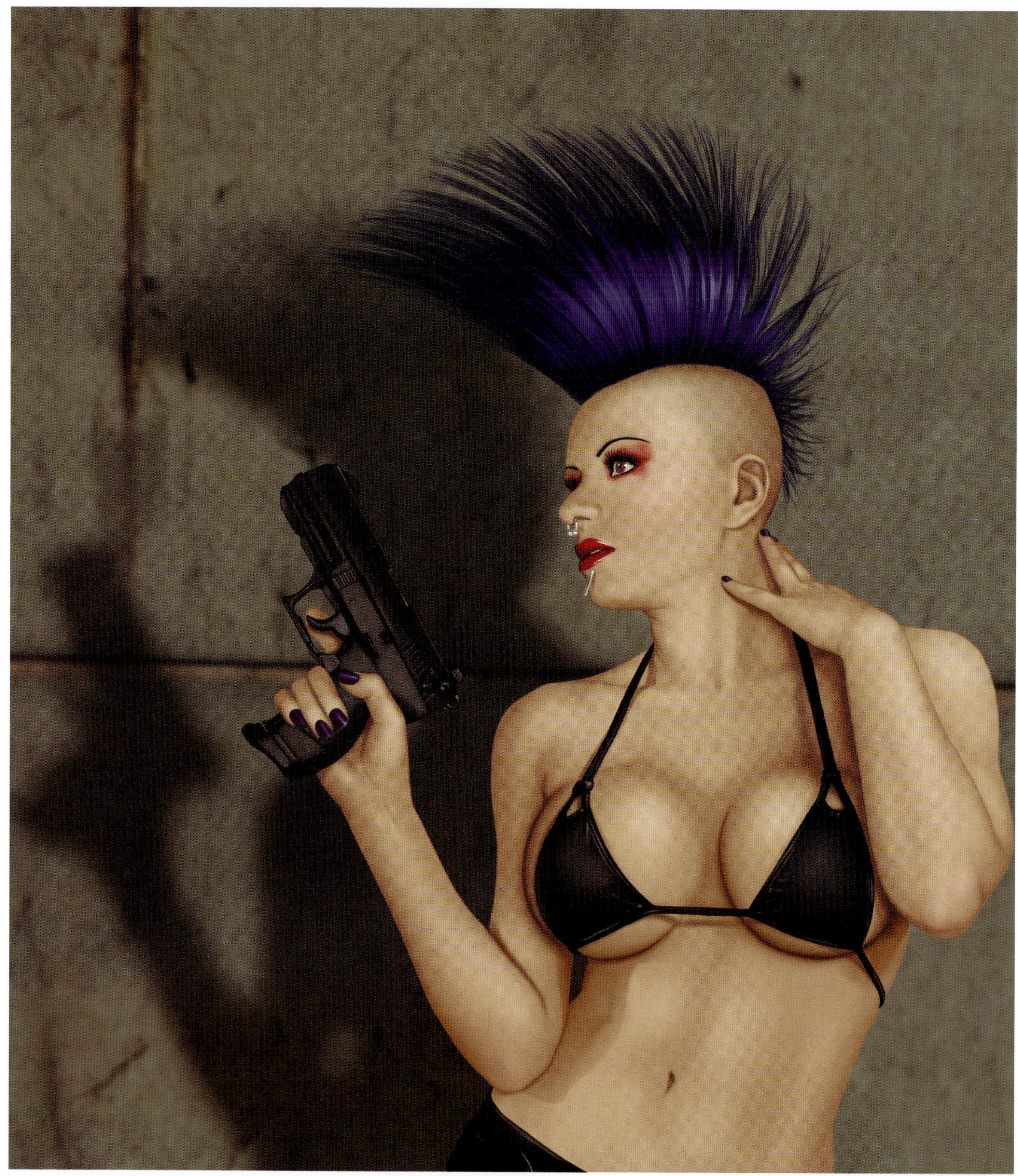

Punkland

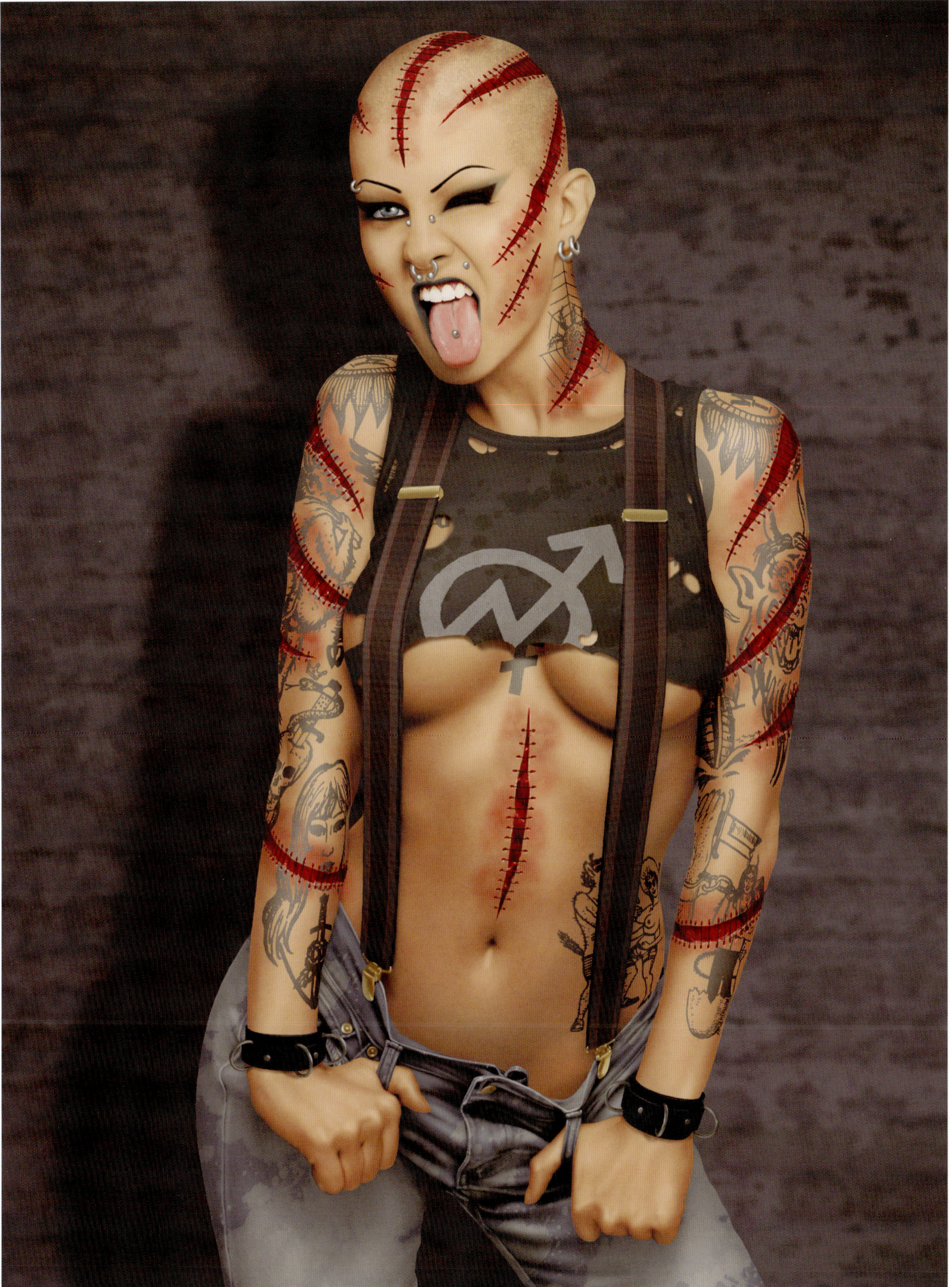

Skinhead Girls

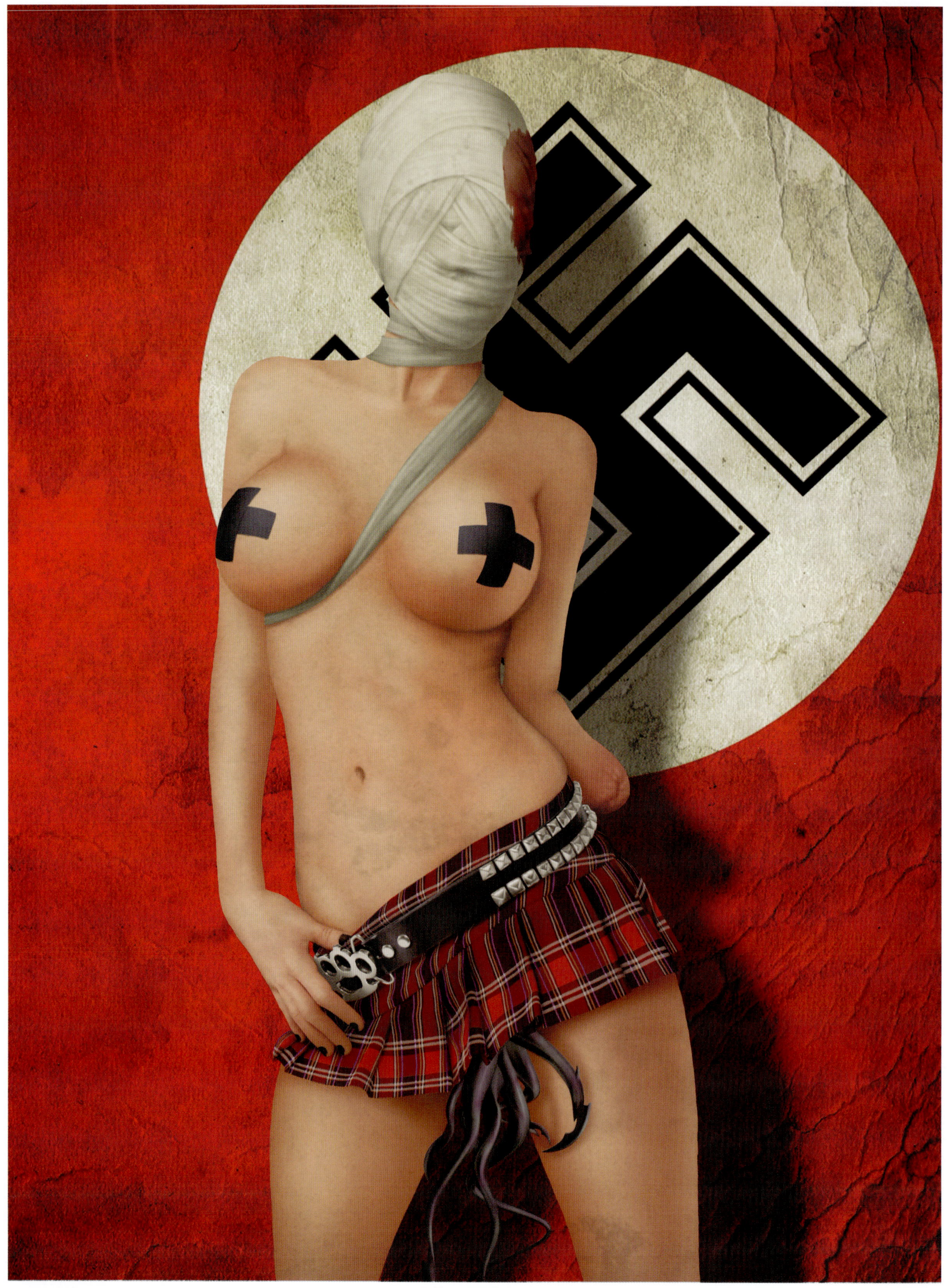

Adolf in Wonderland

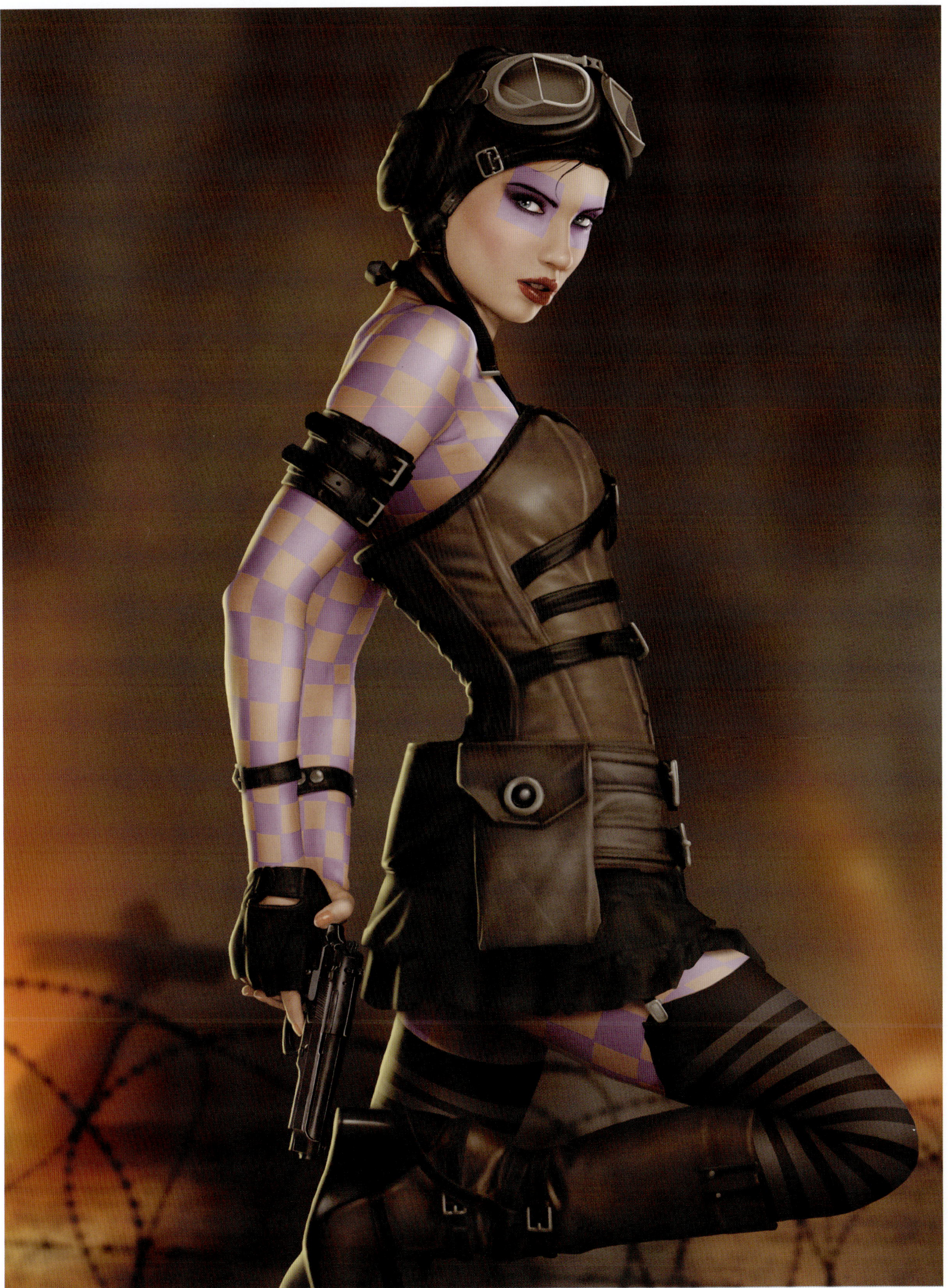

Strike Witches

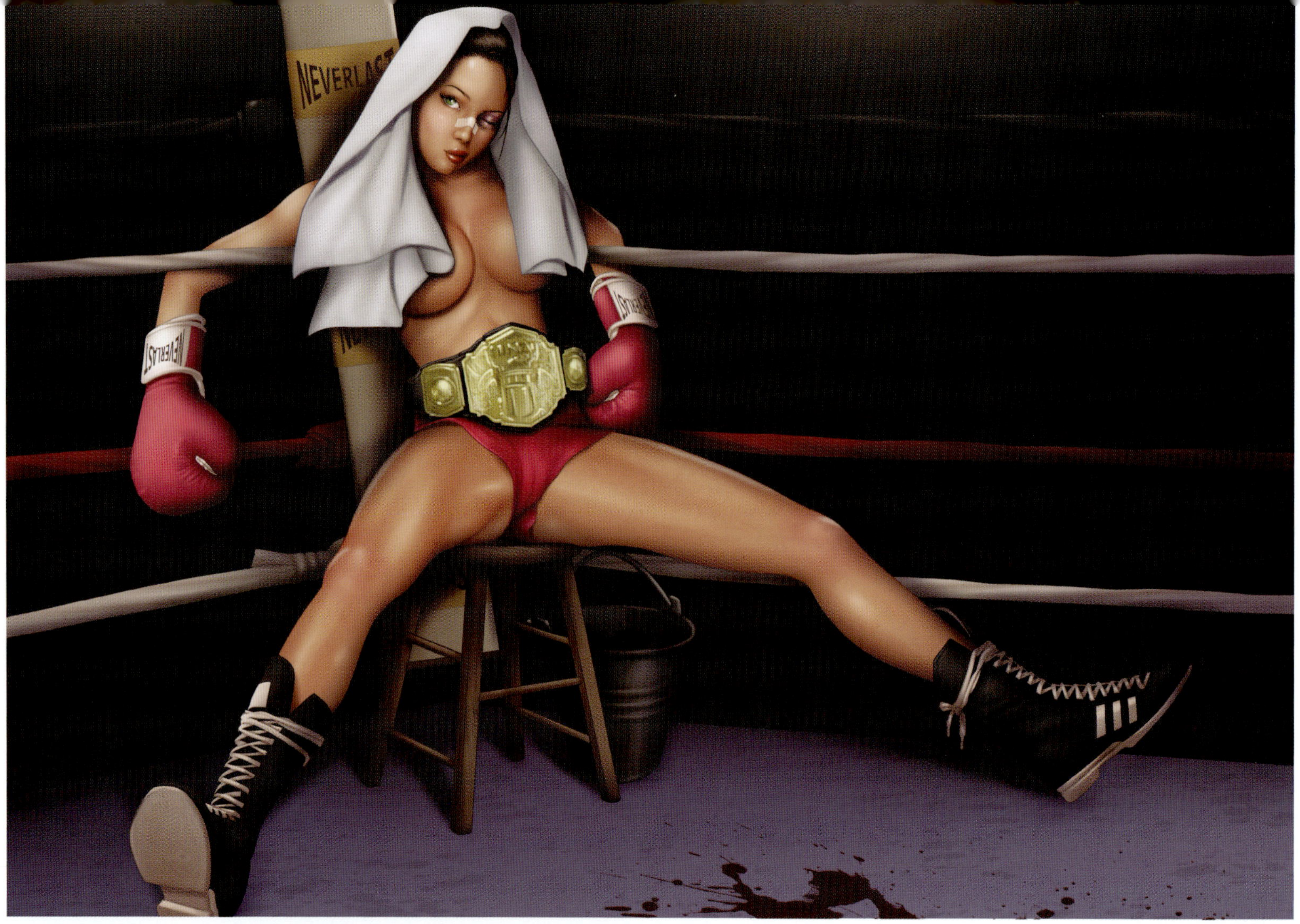

Knockout

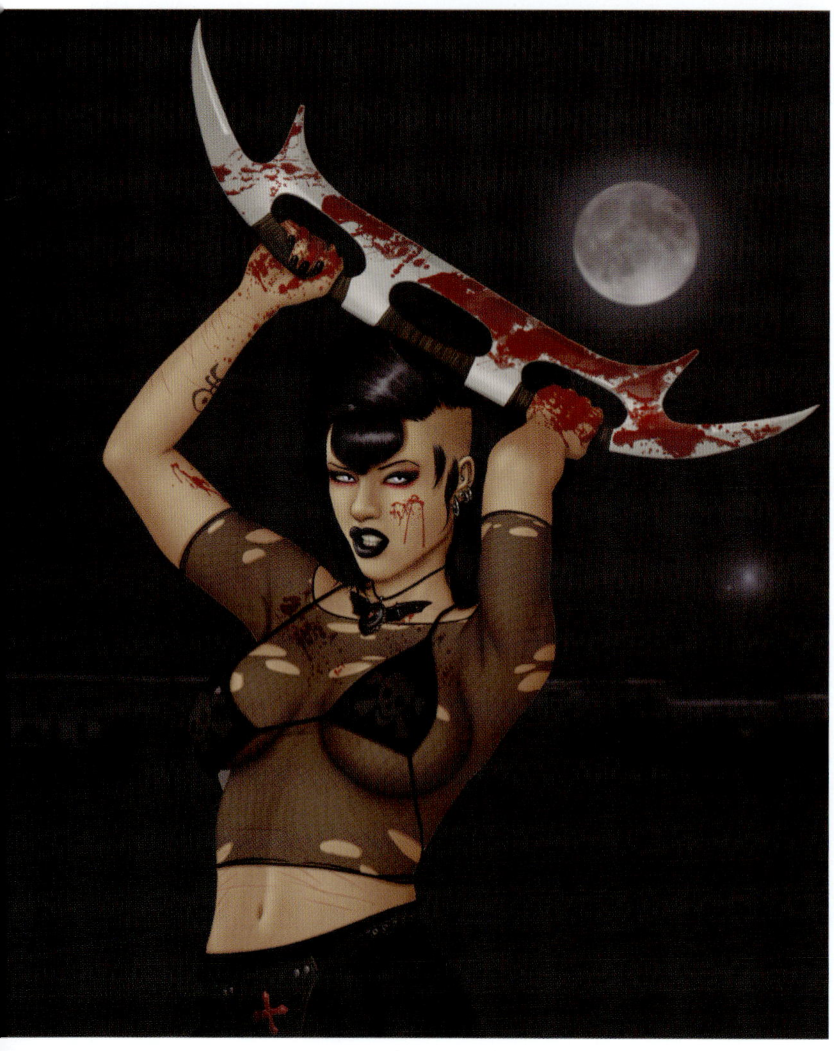

Menstruating Mall

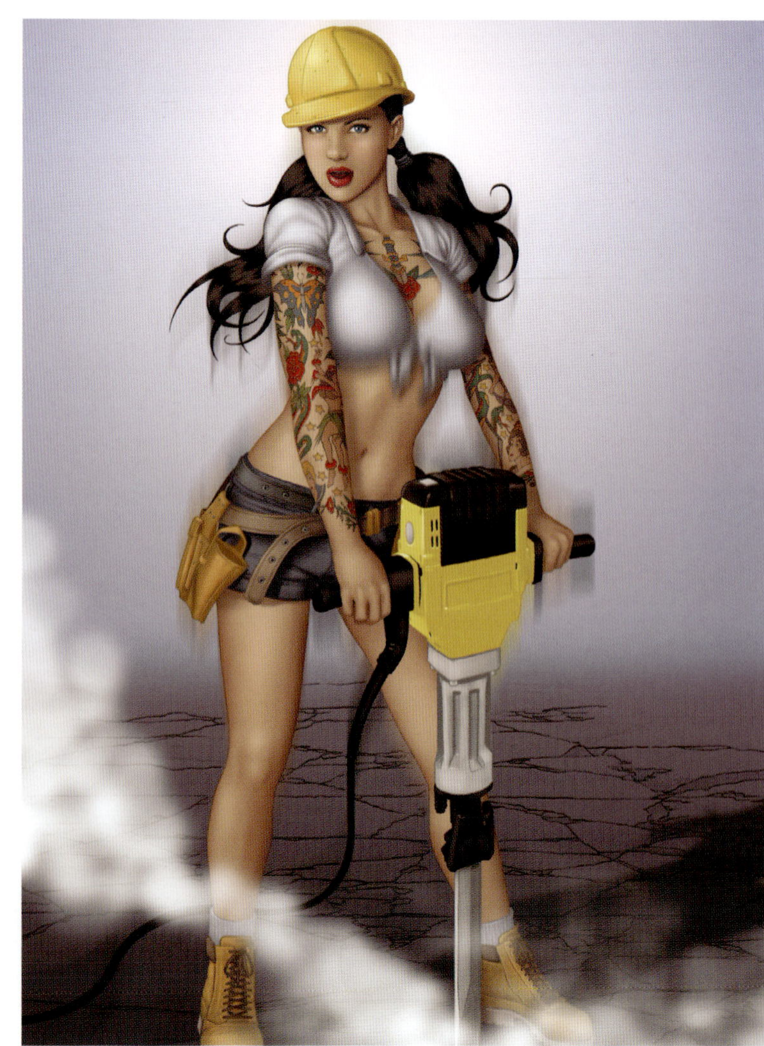

Construction

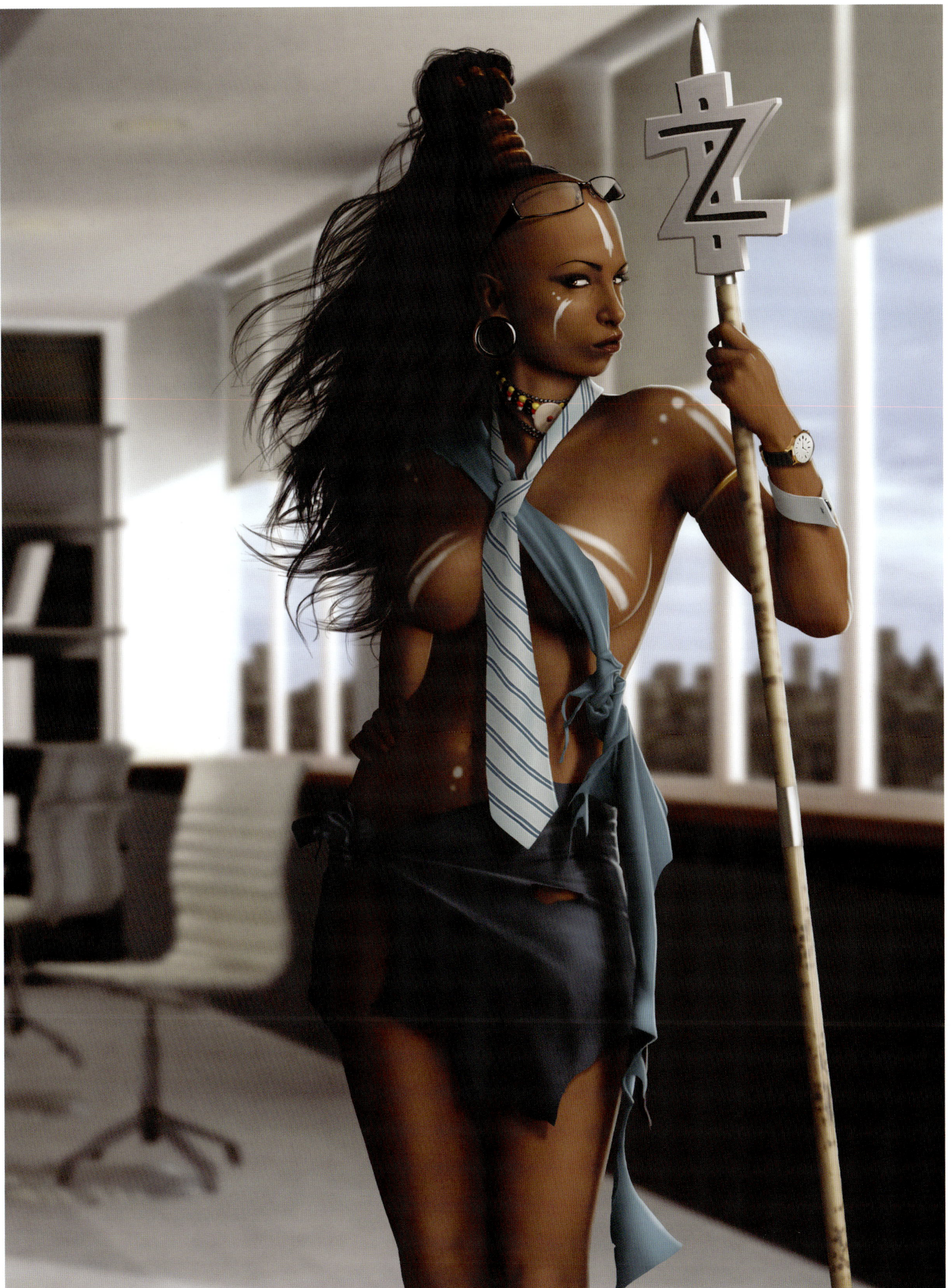

Corporate Zulu

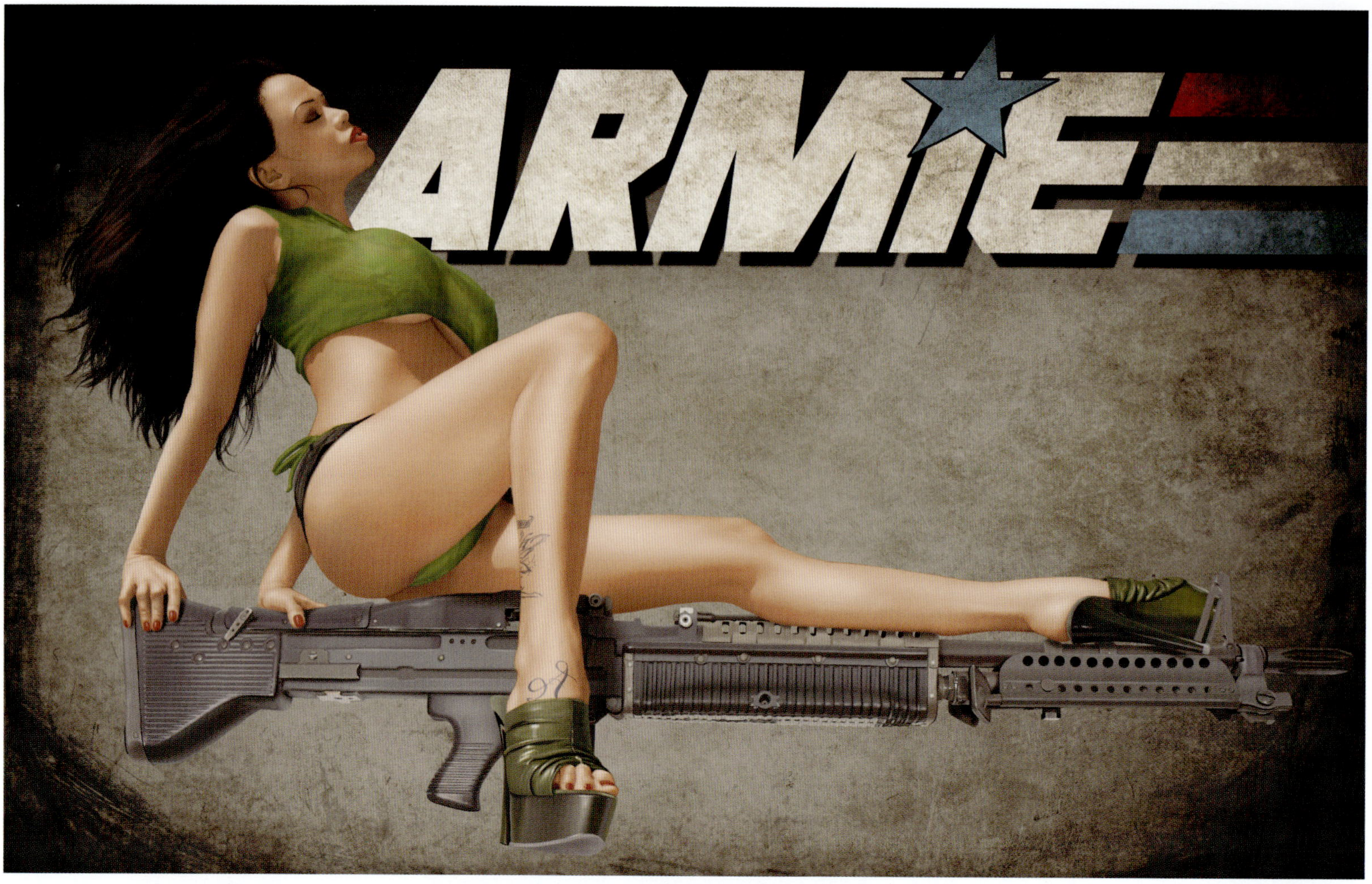

Armie

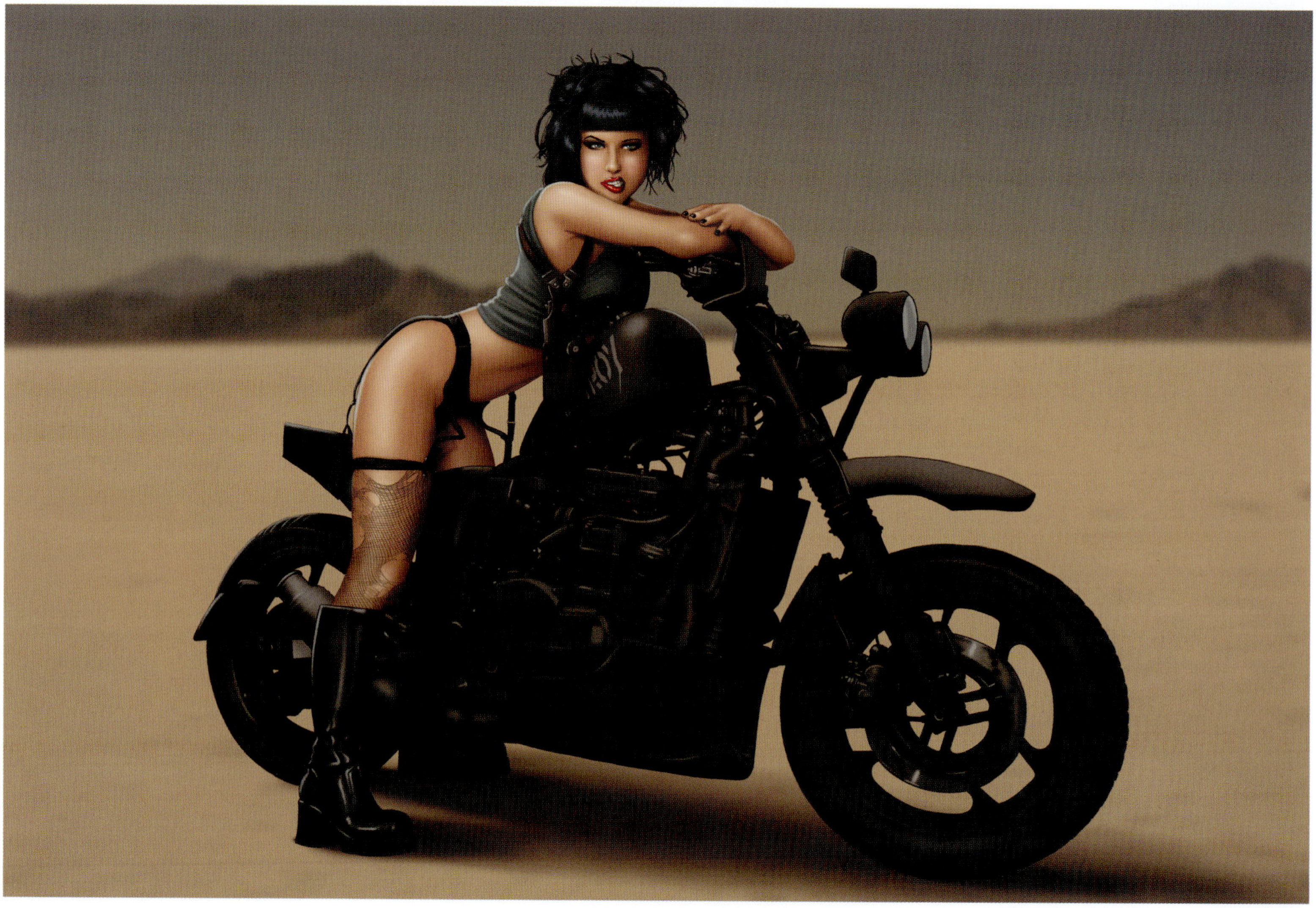

Rat Bike

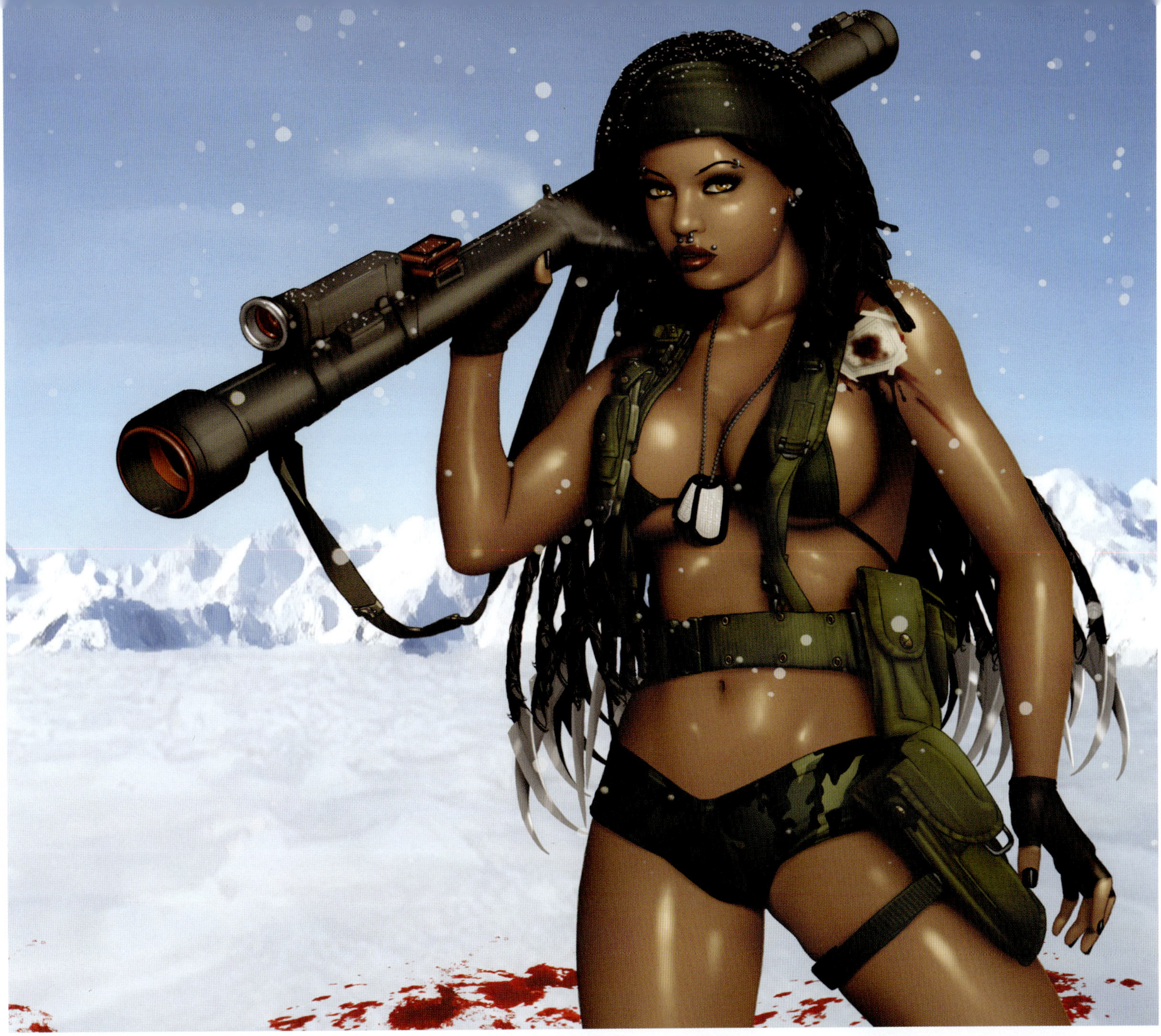

War Slut

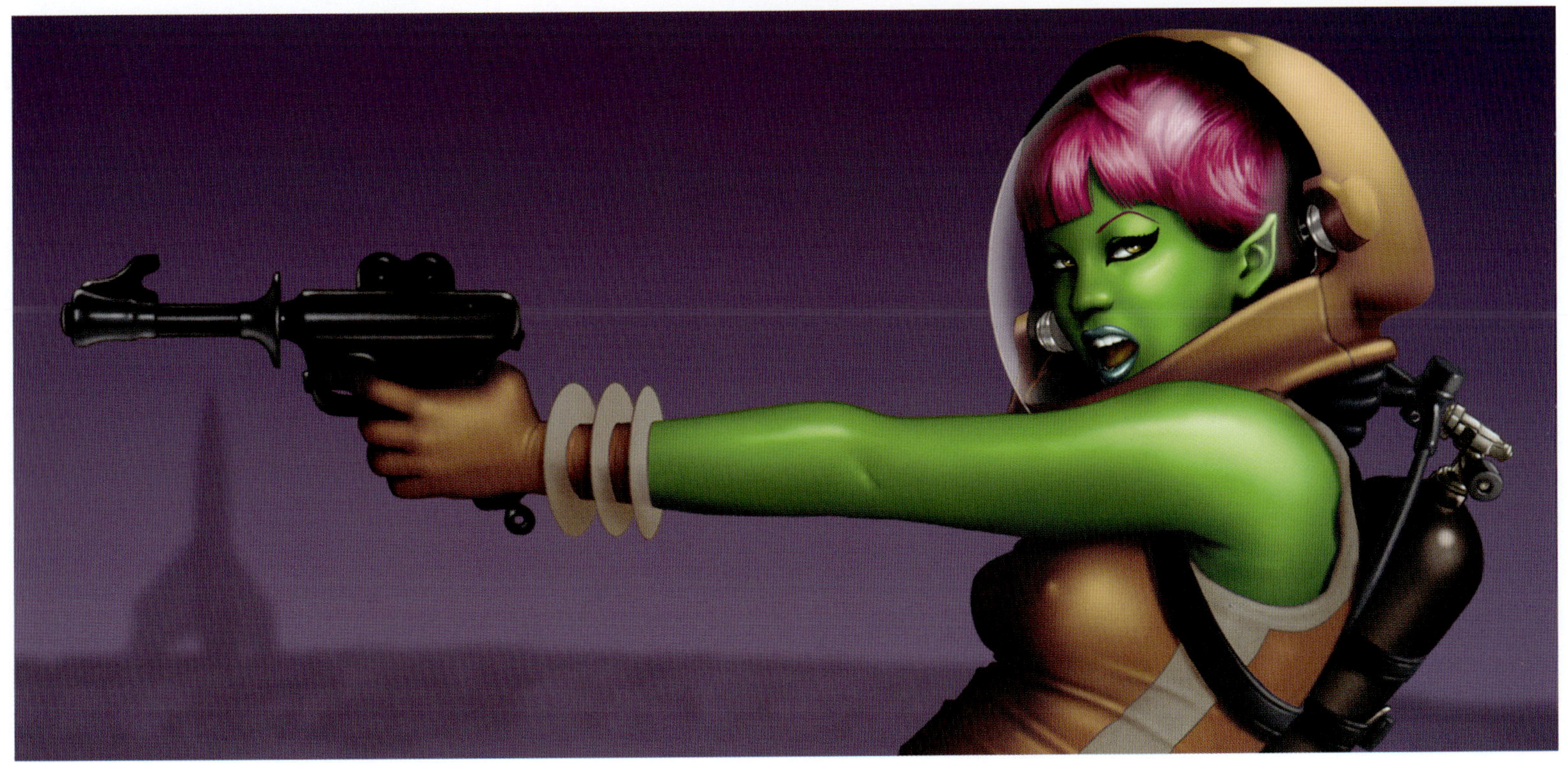

Space Chick

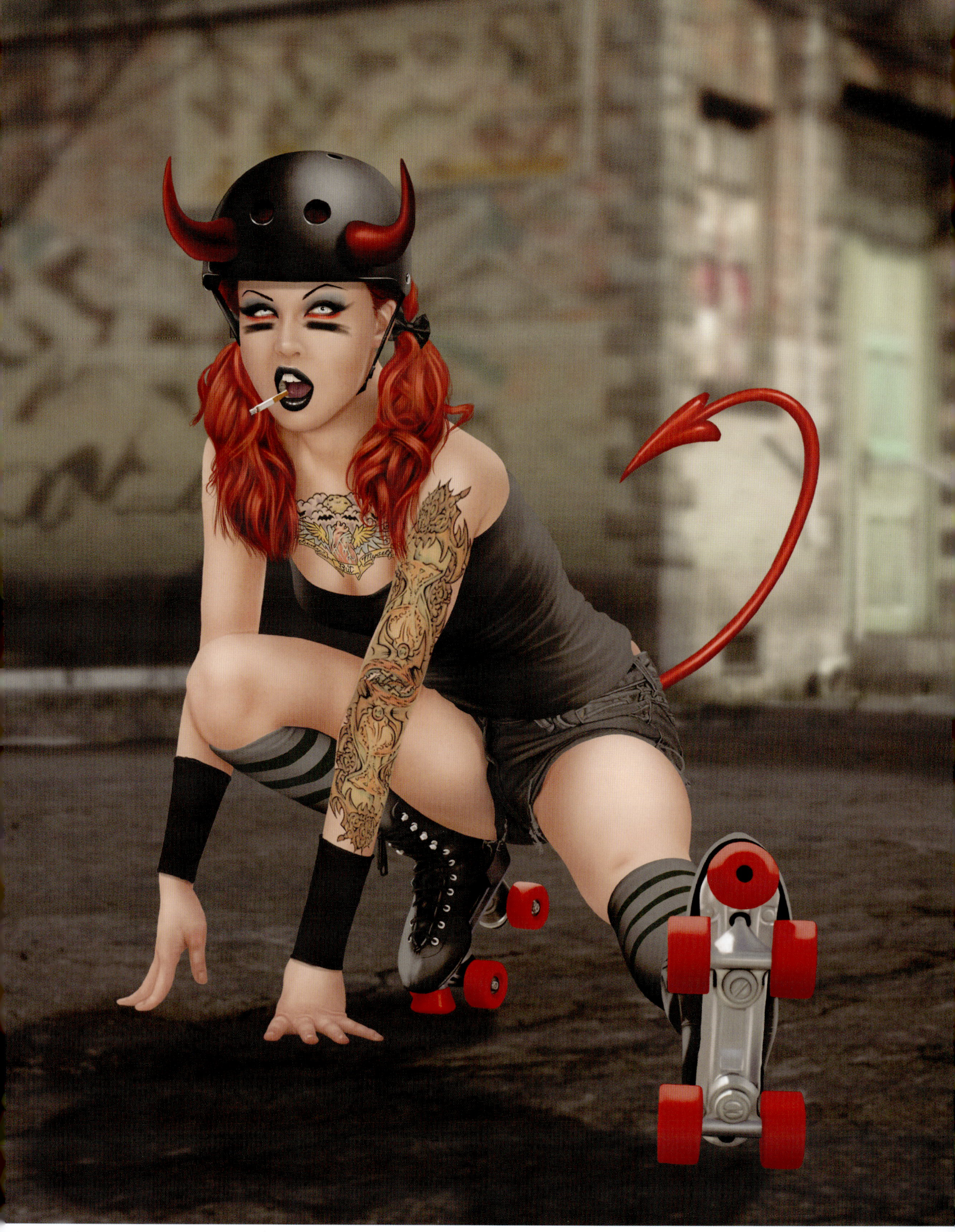

Roller Derby

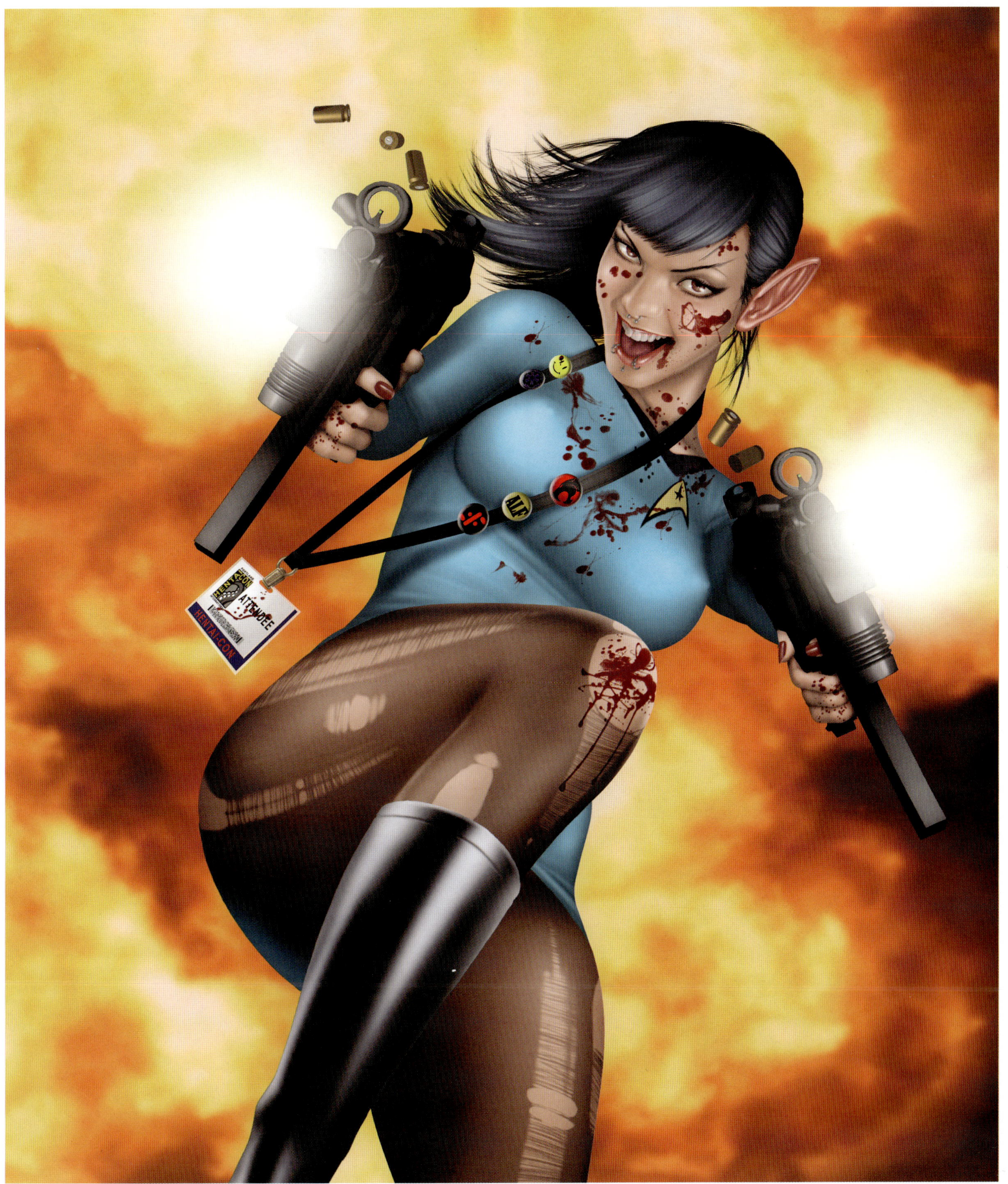

Nerd Rage

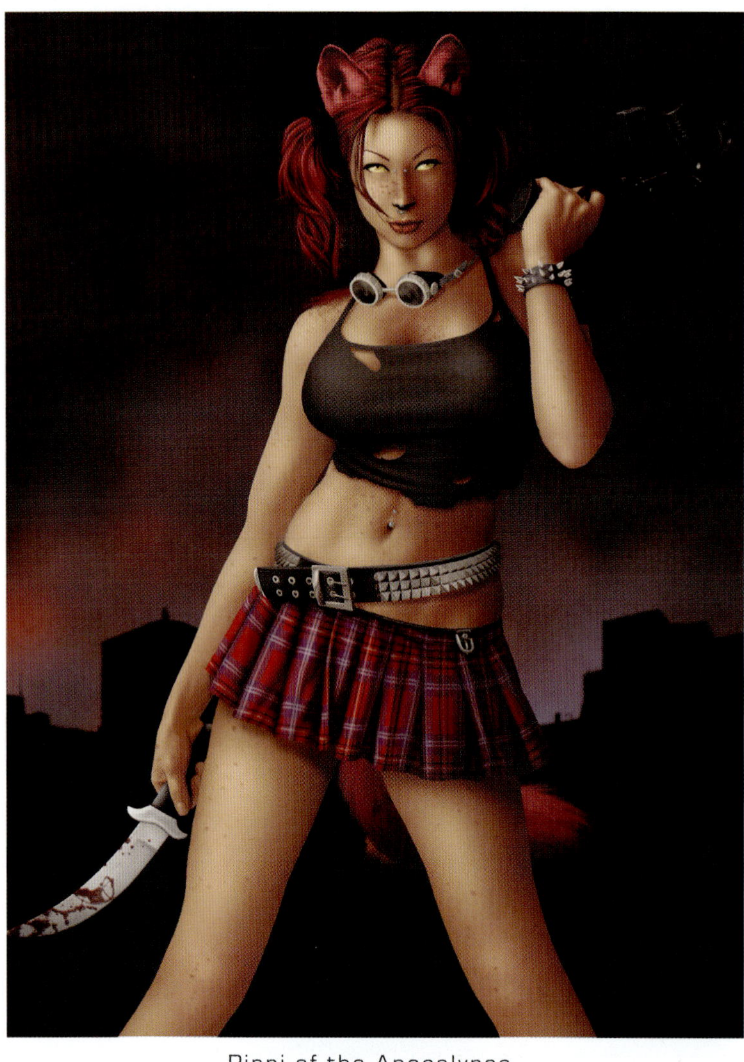

Pippi of the Apocalypse

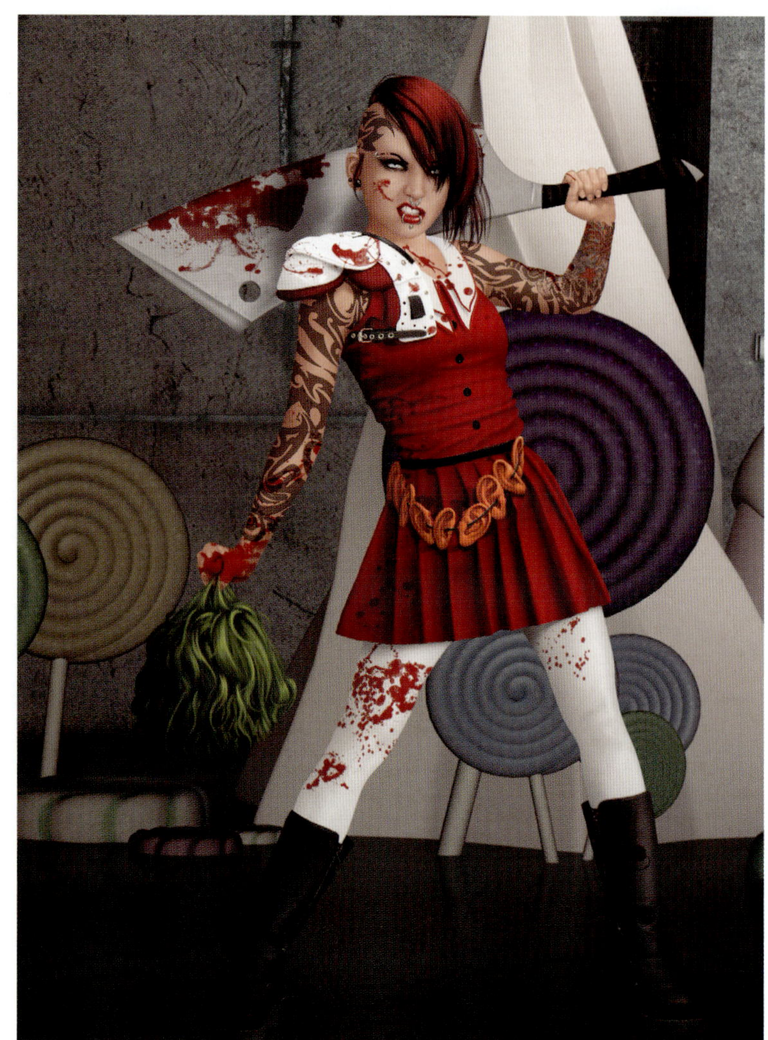

Wonka

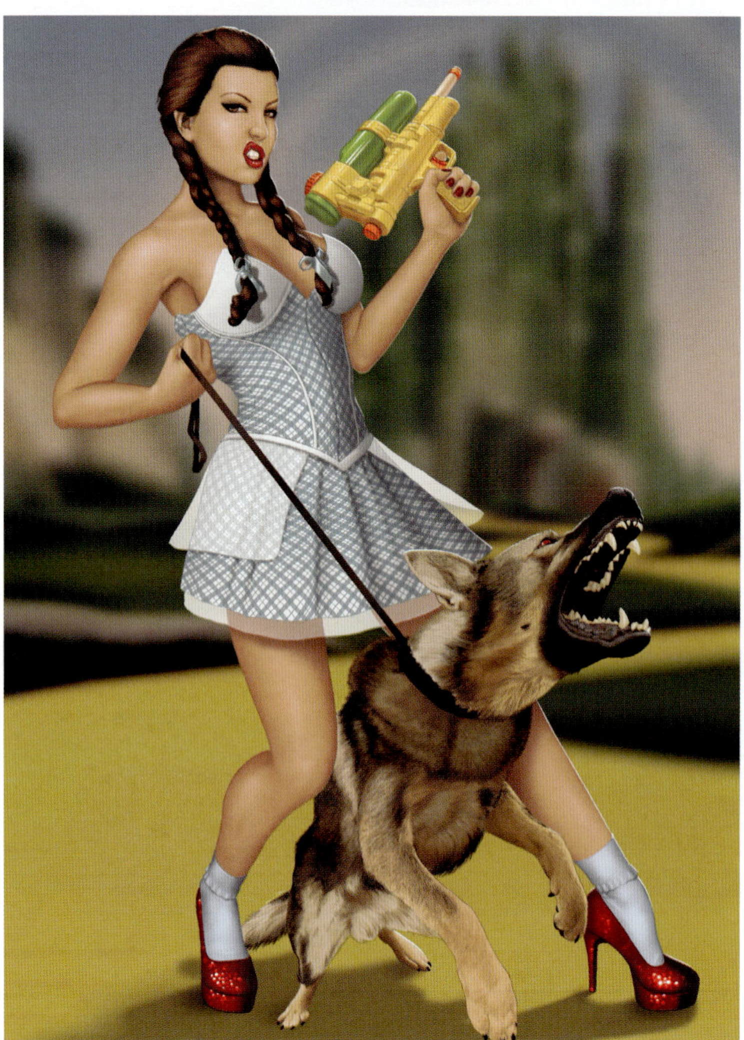

Dorothy 2000

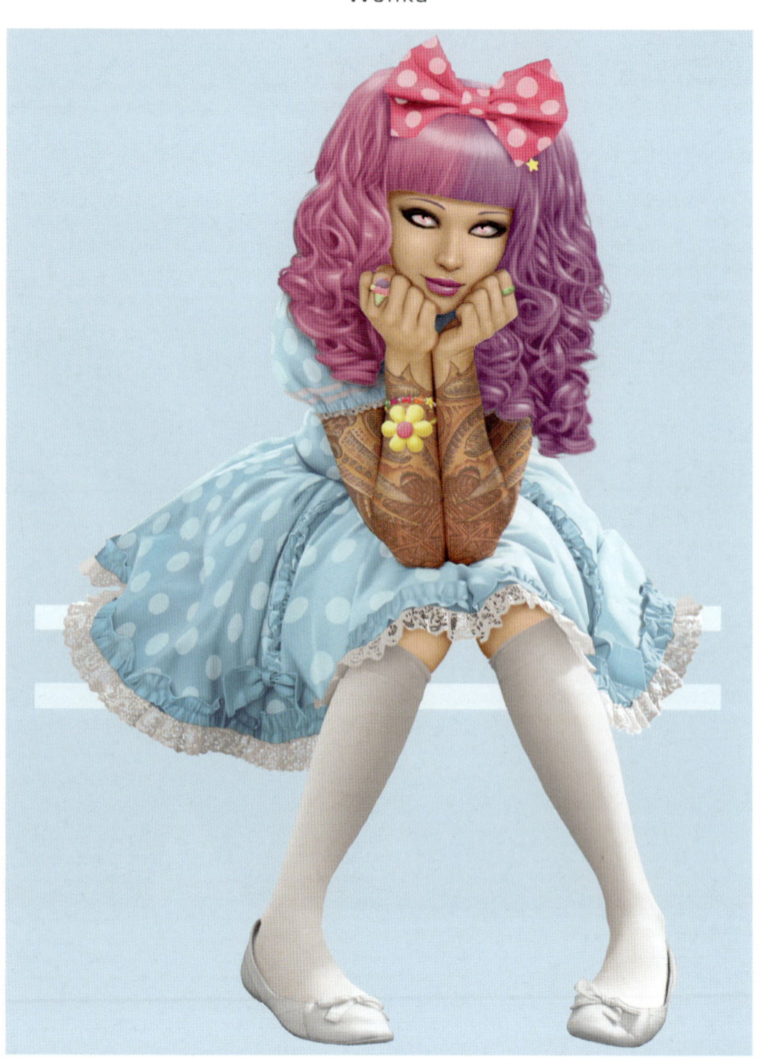

Lolita

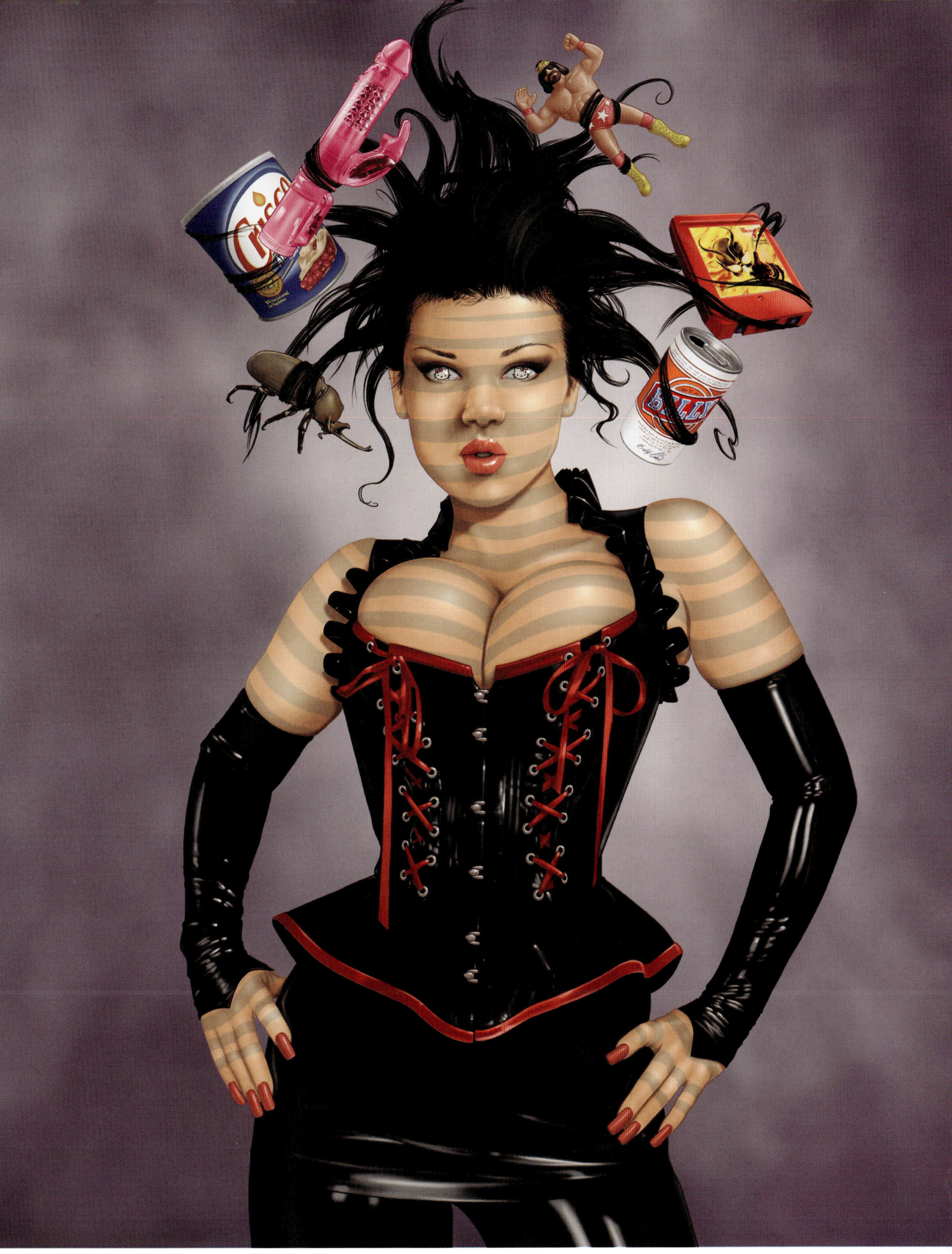

Fantastic Orgy

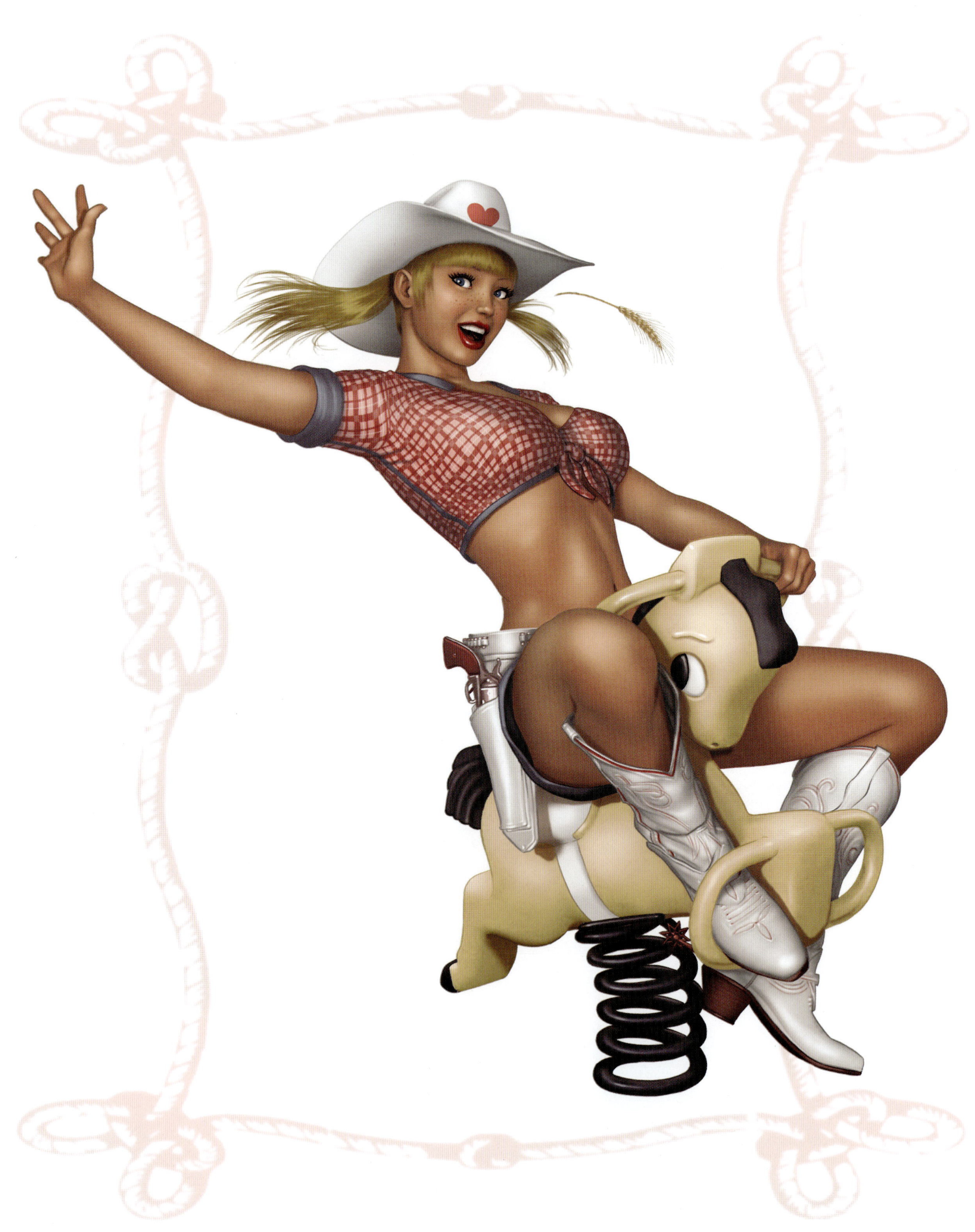

Cowgirl

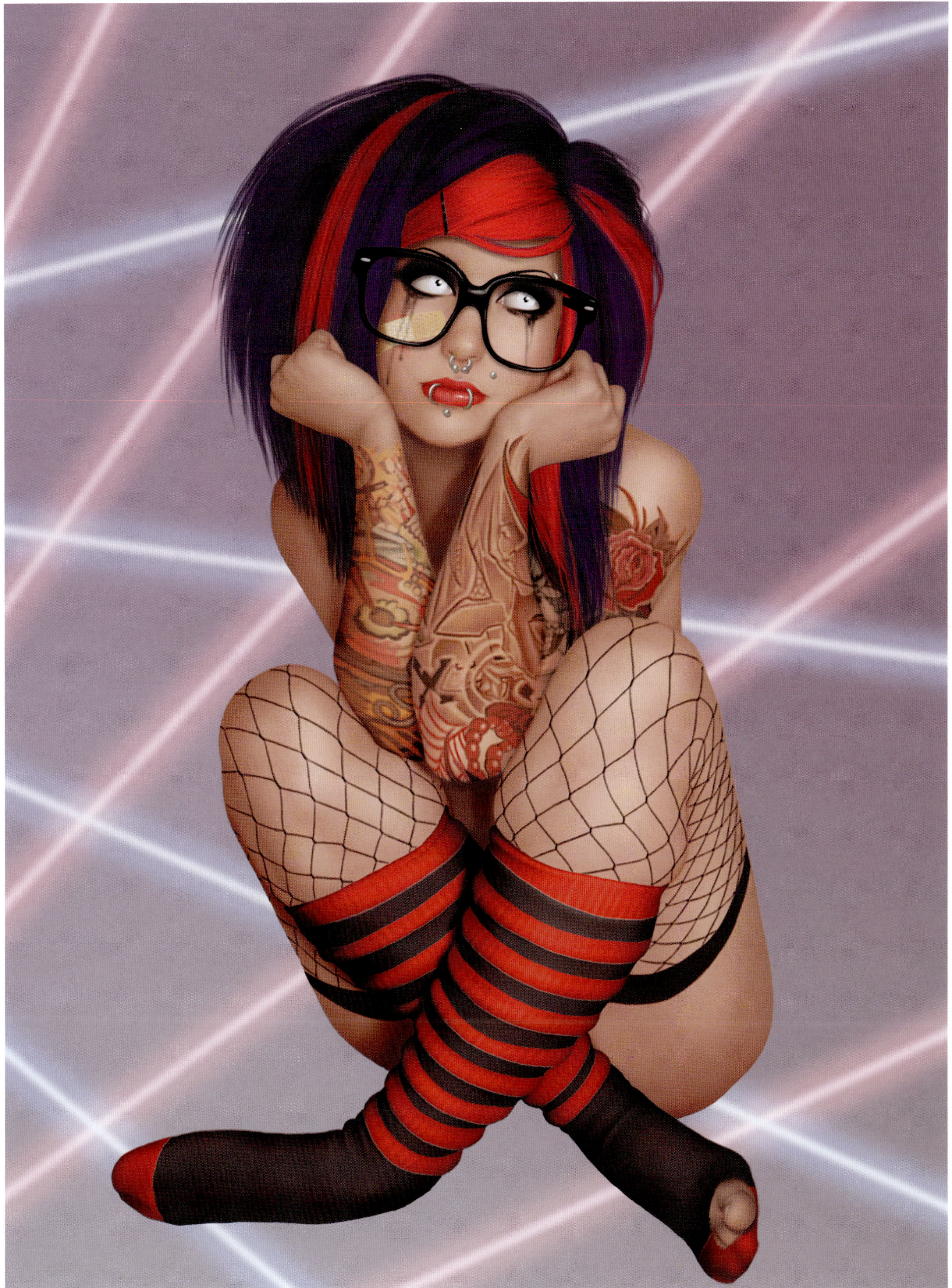

Scene

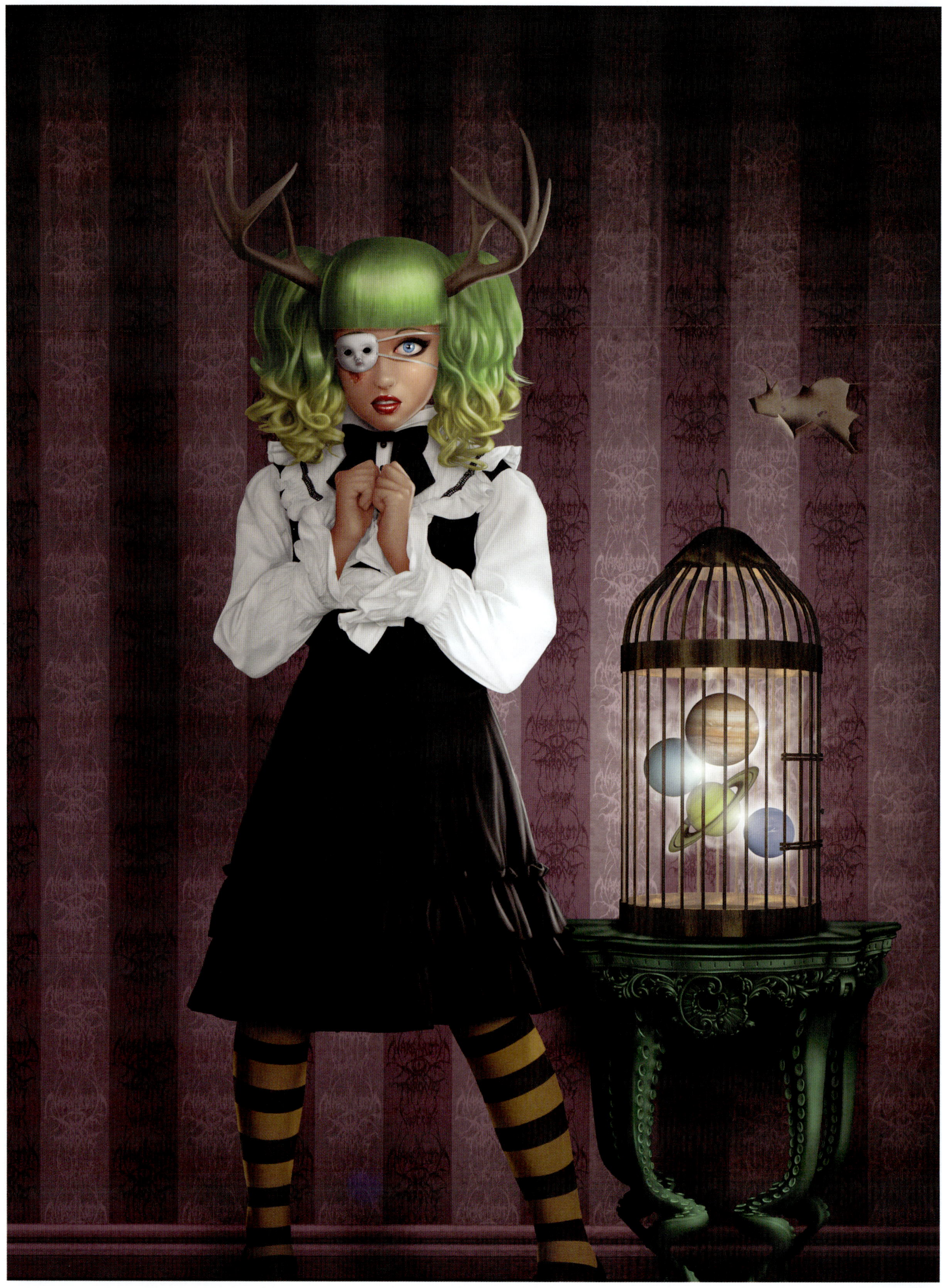

Quicksand House

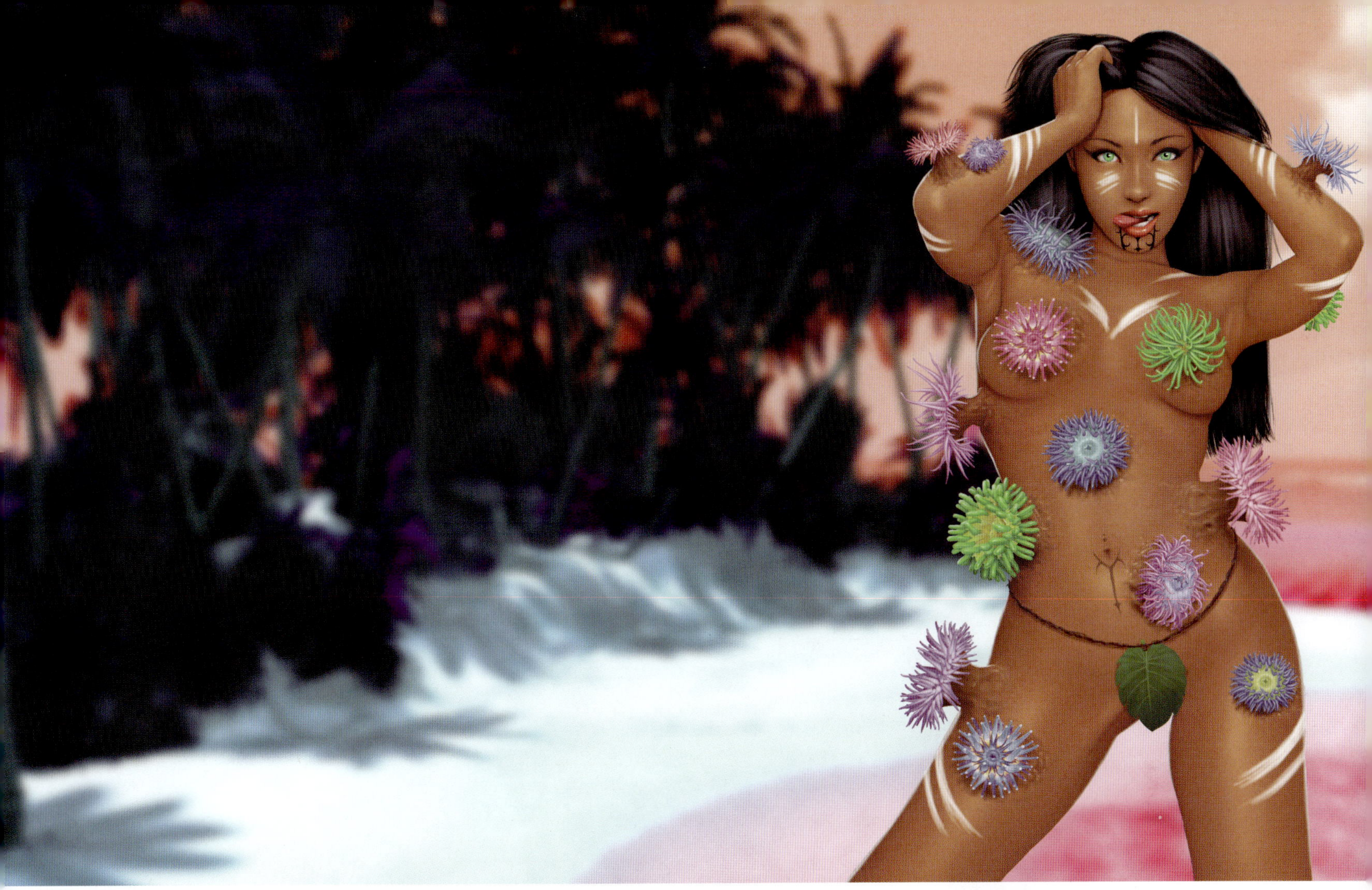

Desert Island

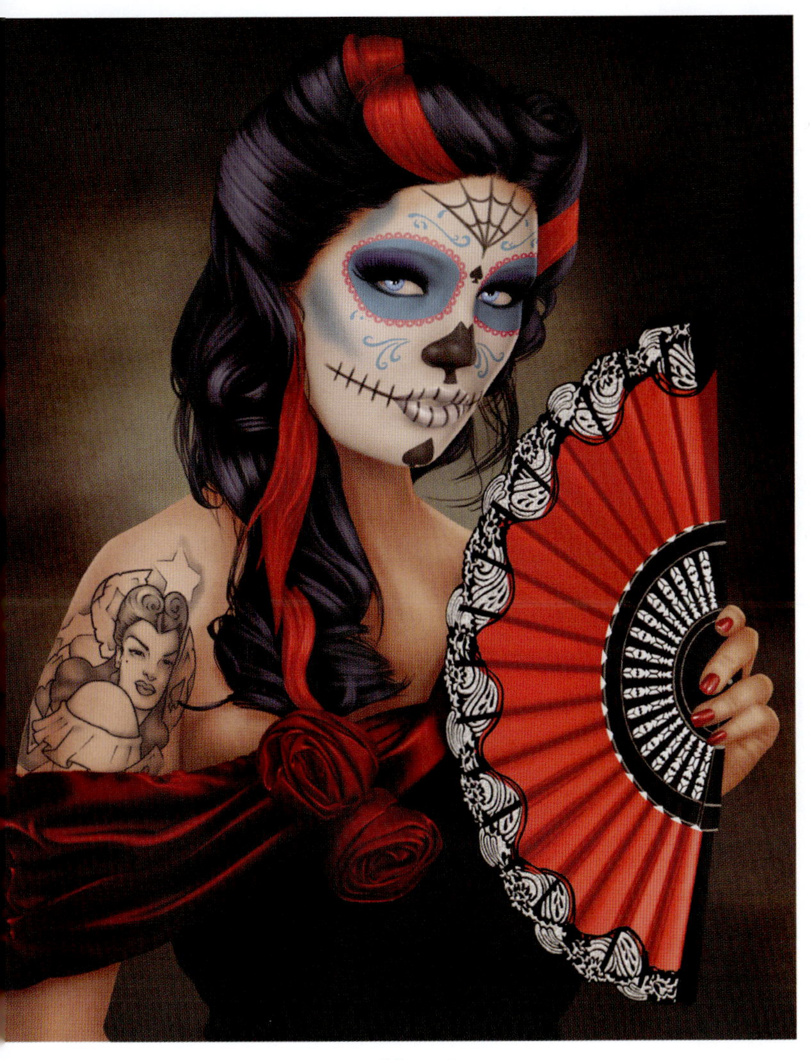

Muerte

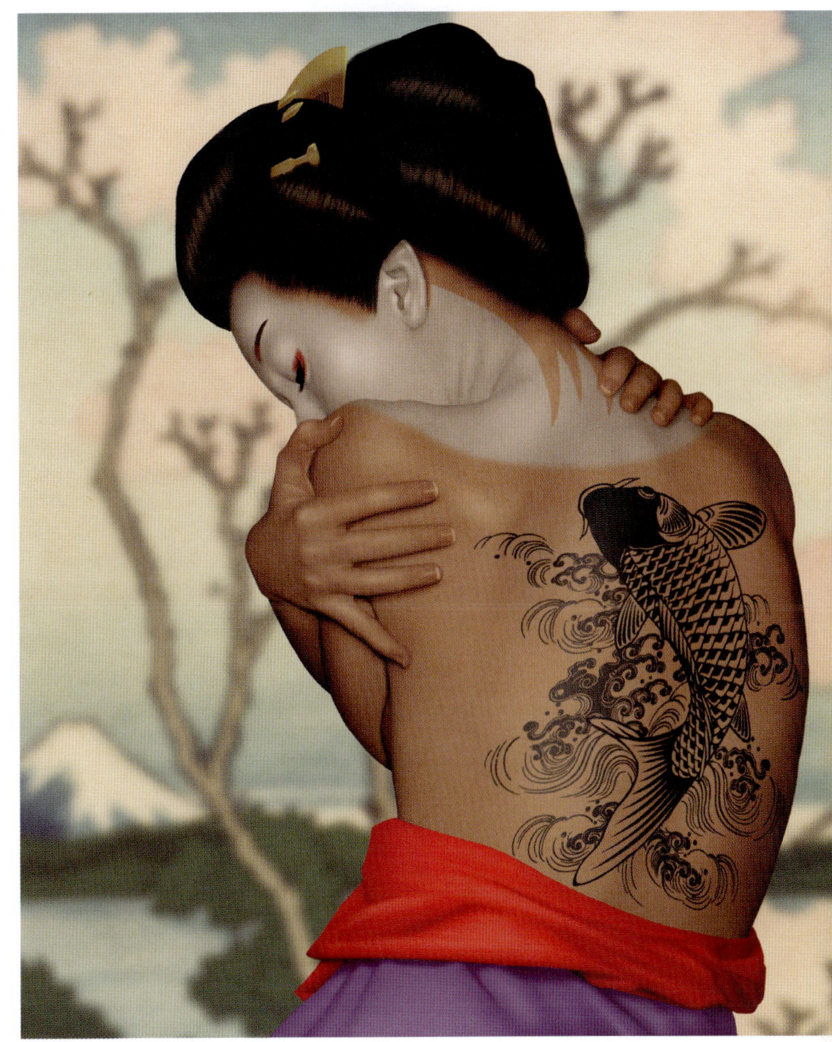

Geisha

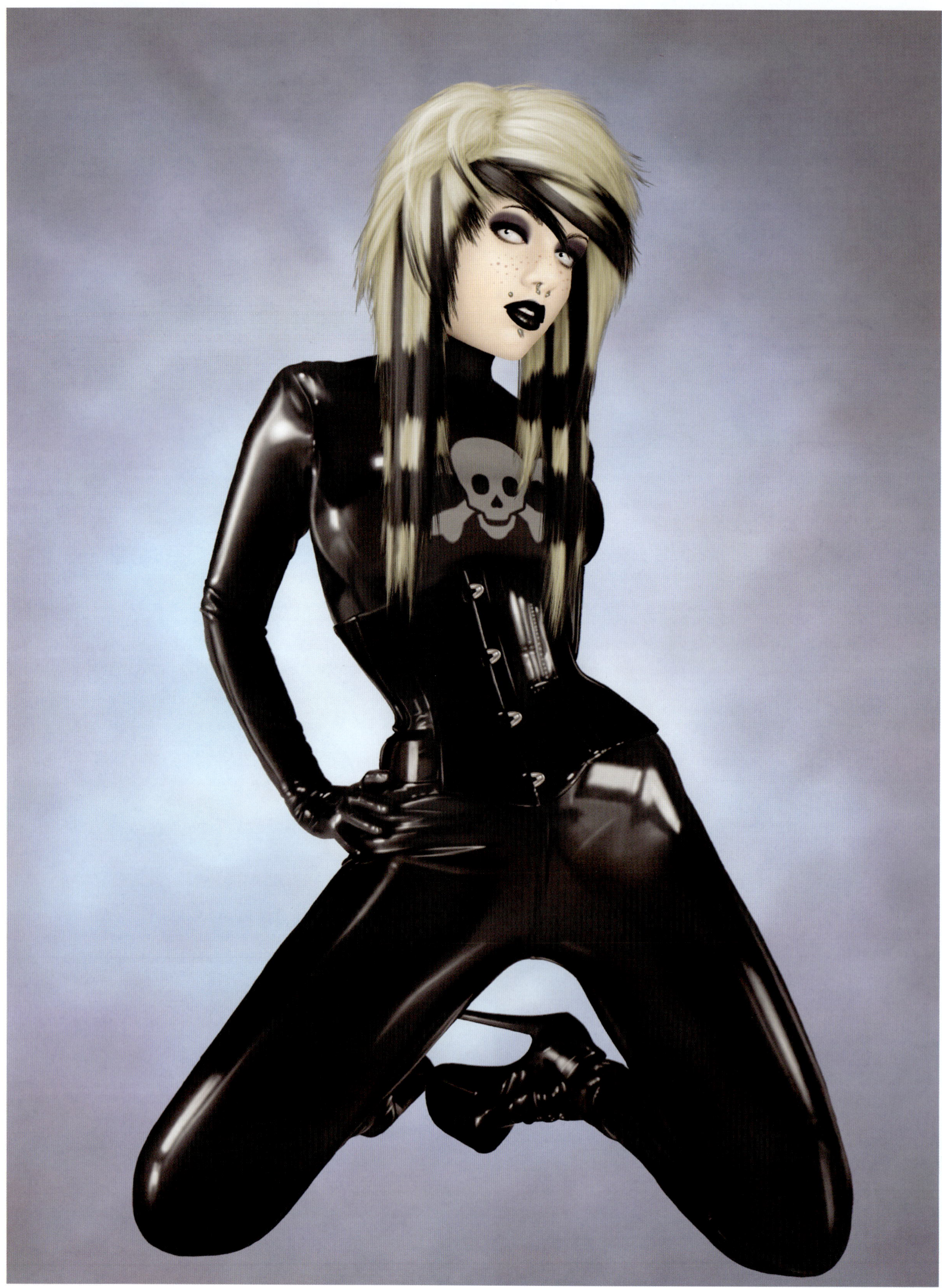

Pirate

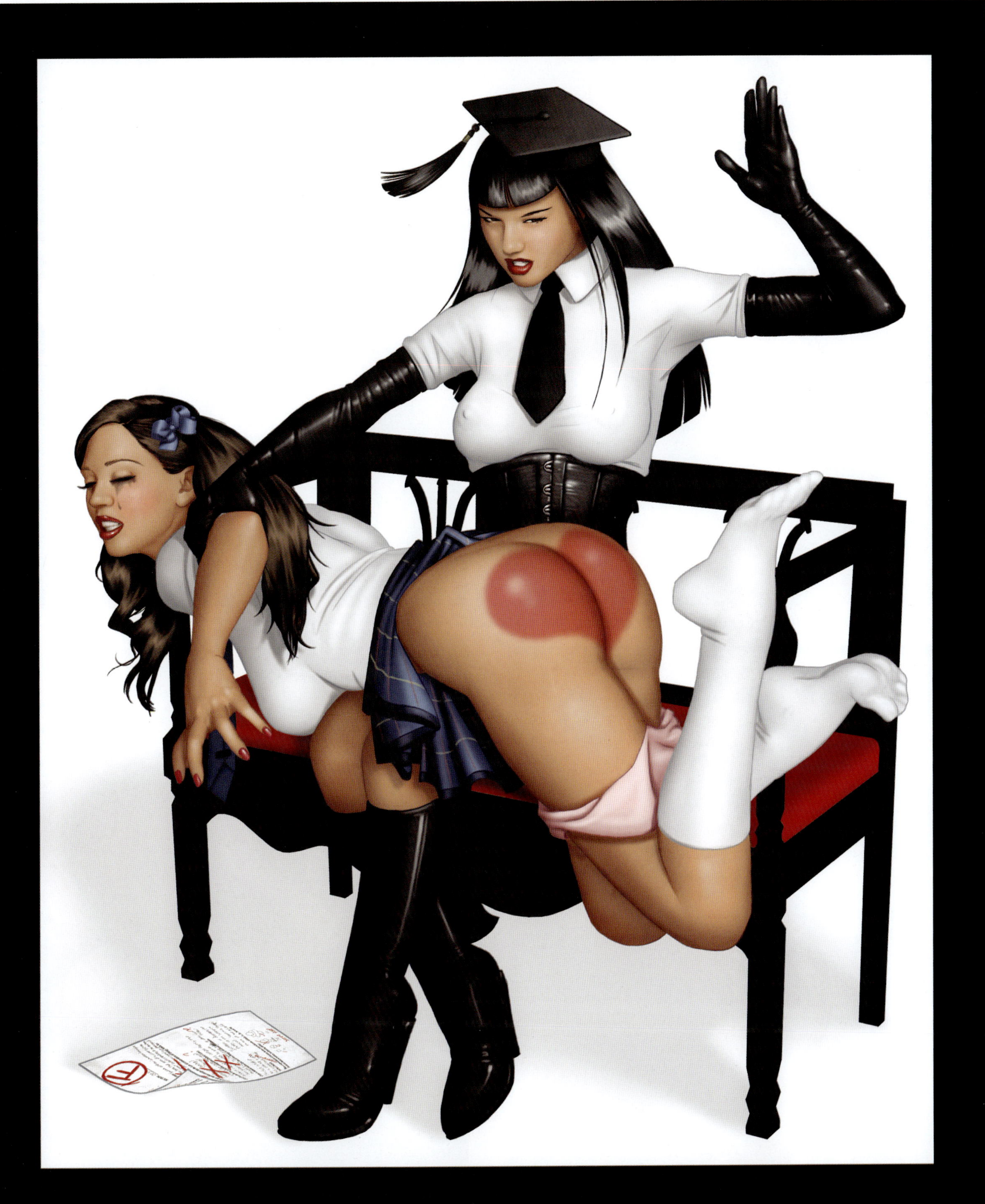

Pleasure Principal

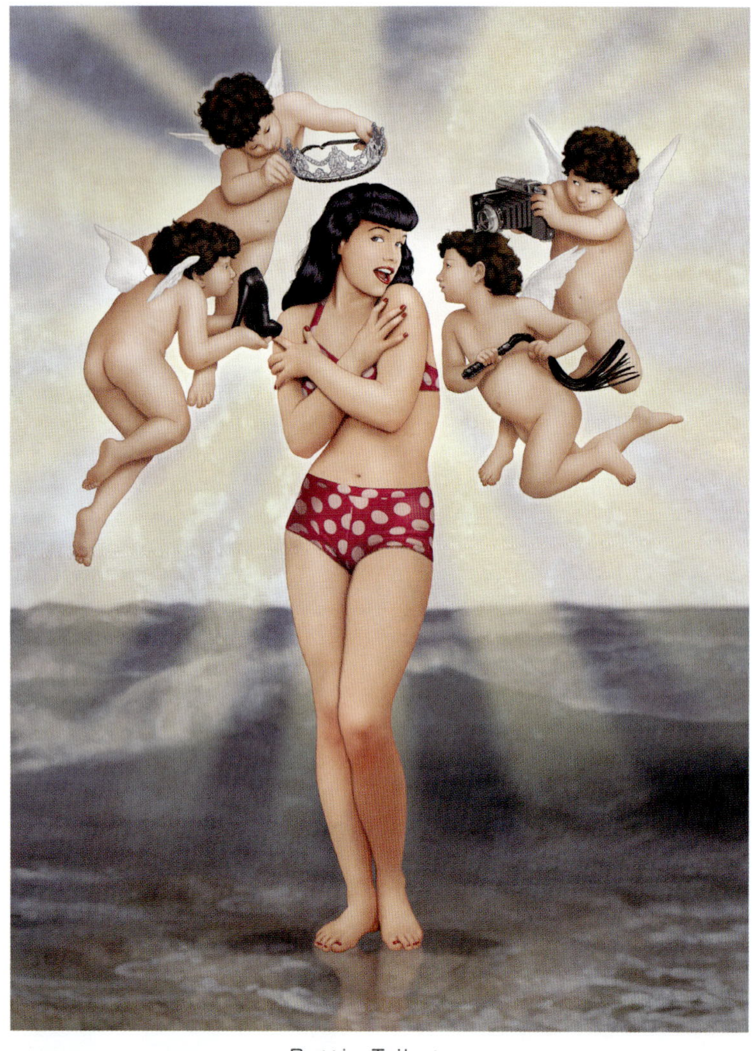
Bettie Tribute

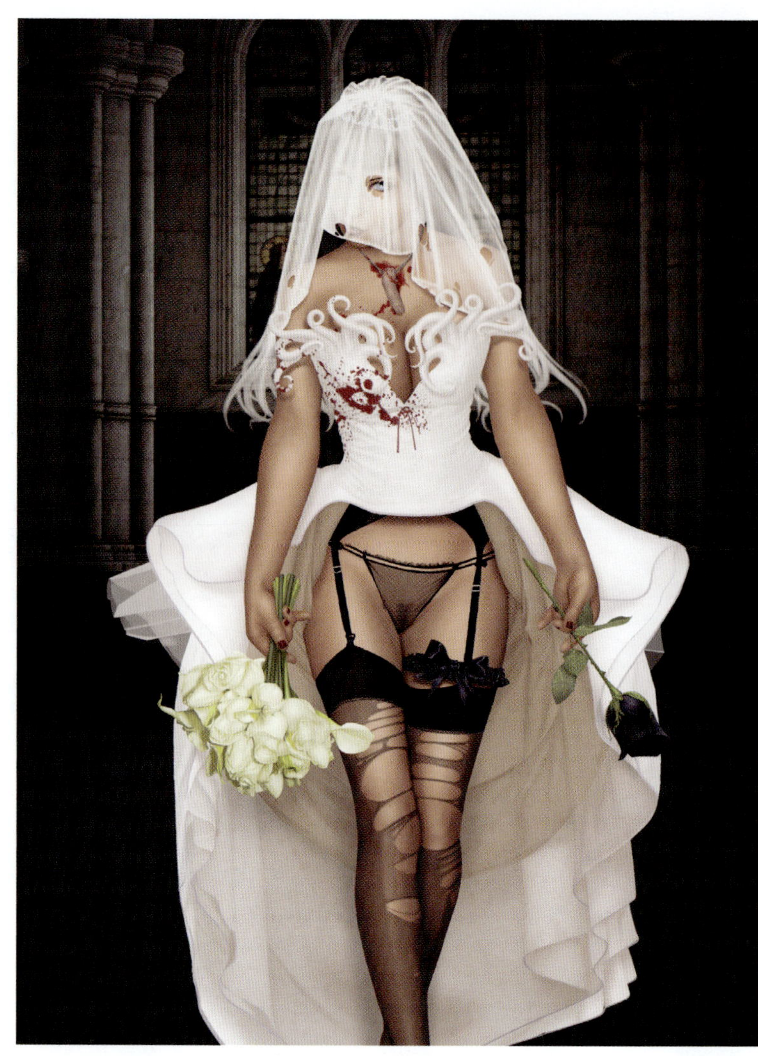
Handsome Squirm

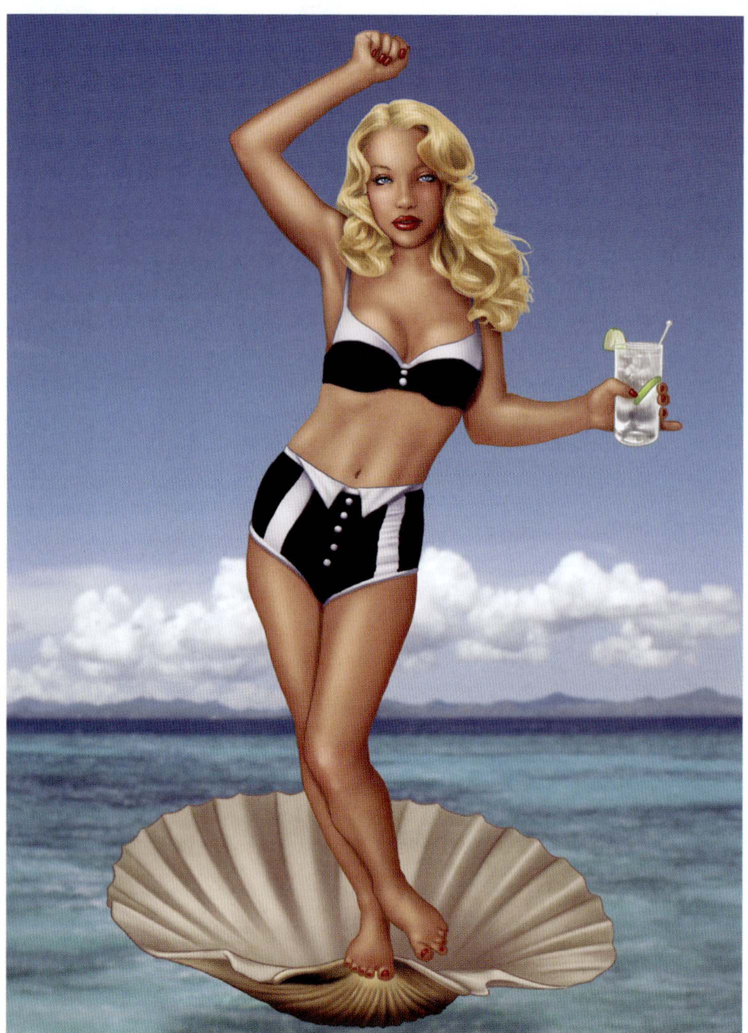
Venus

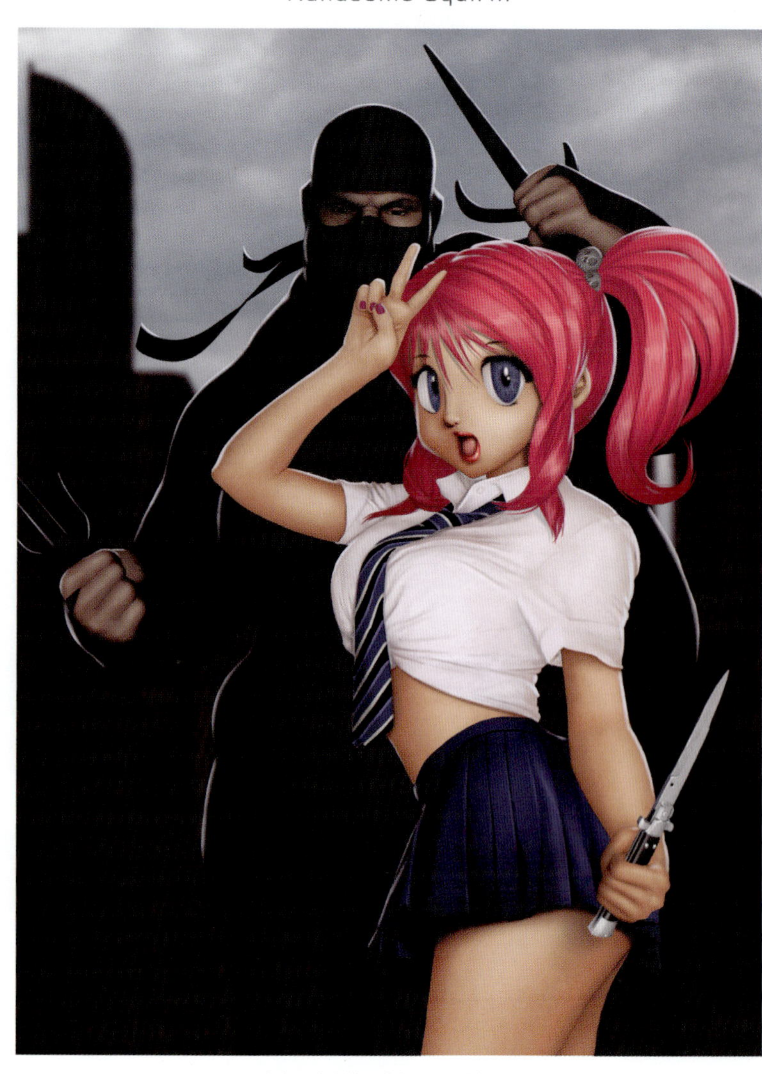
Morbidly Obese Ninja

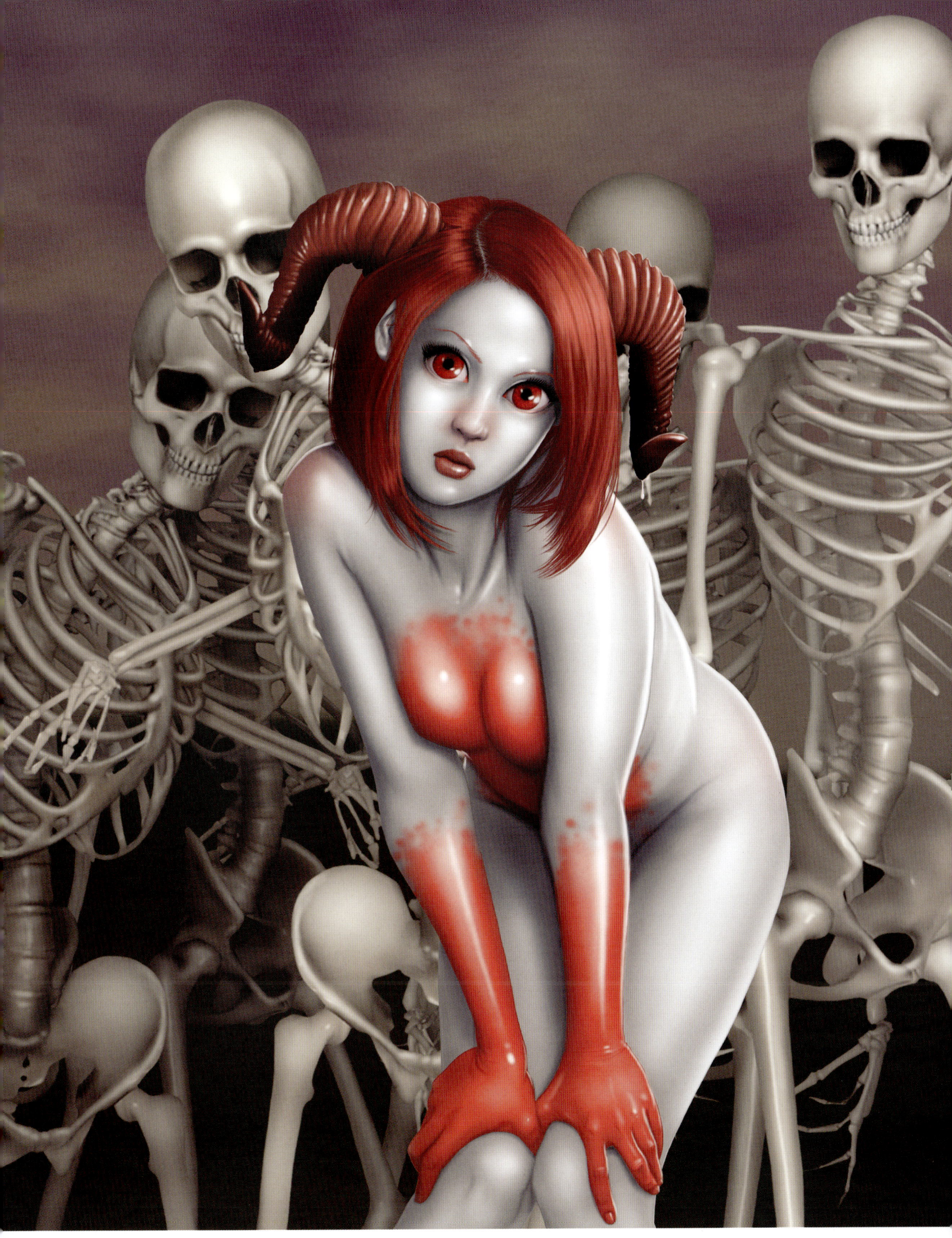

Haunted Vagina

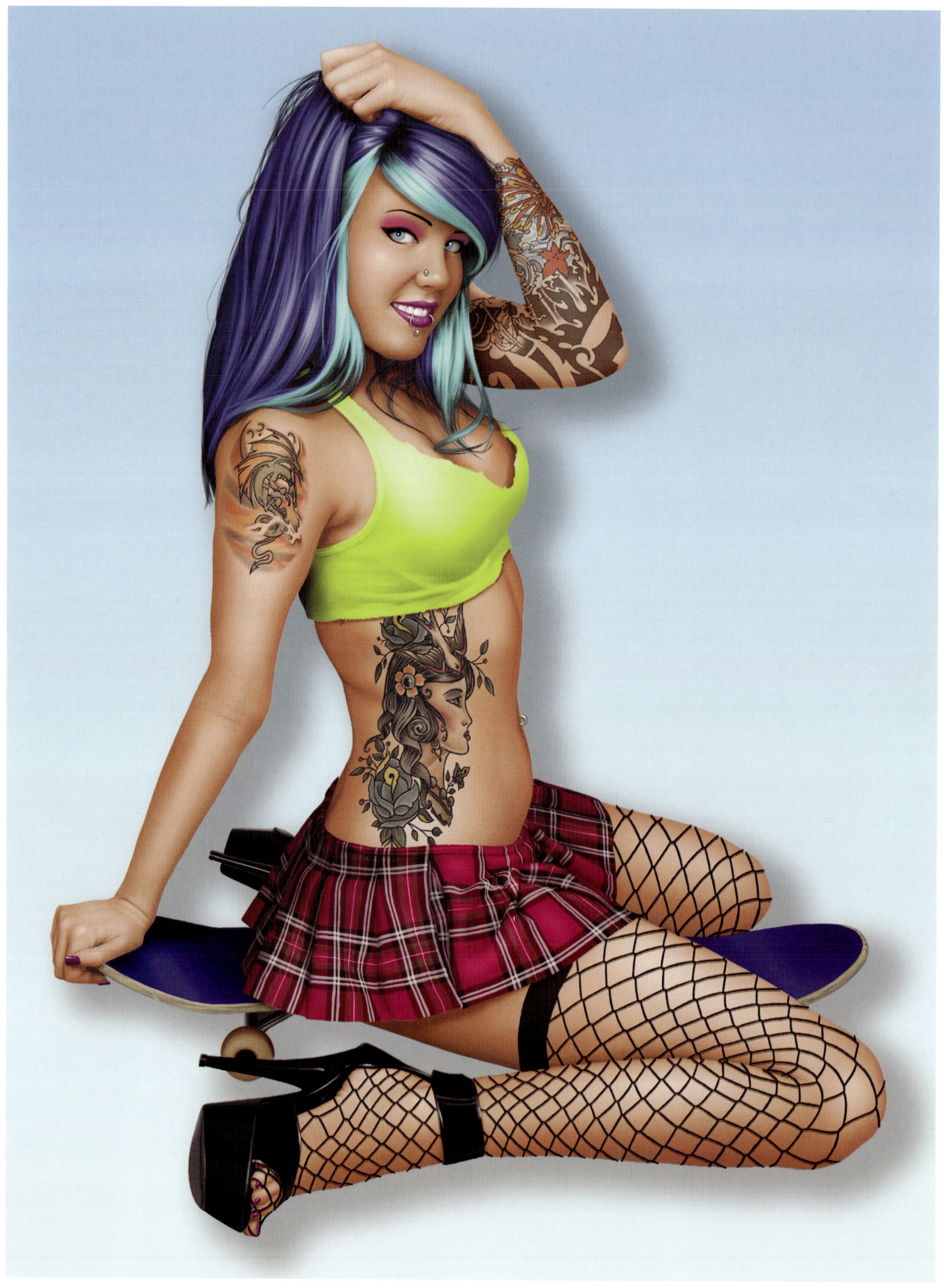

Skateboard

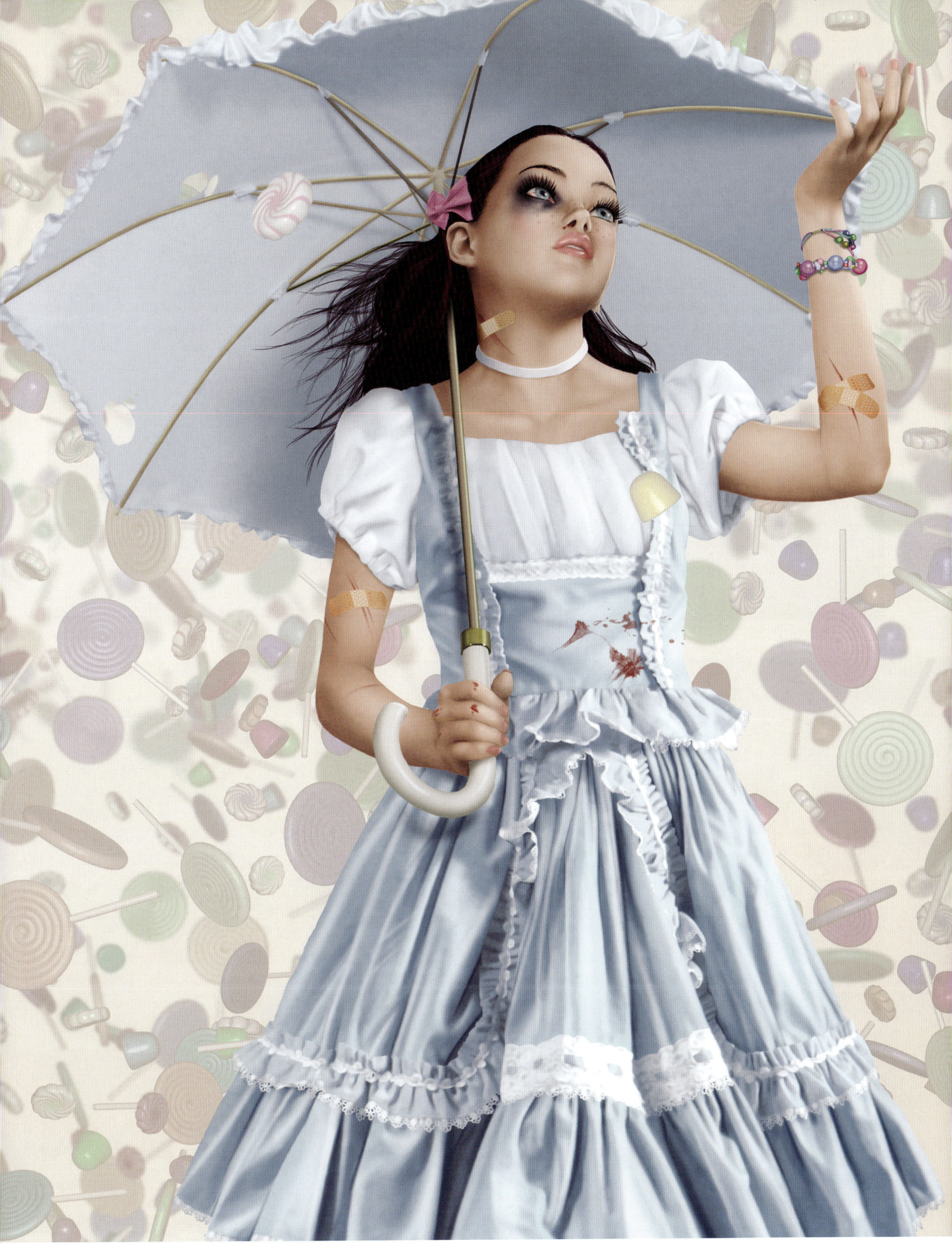

Sweet Story

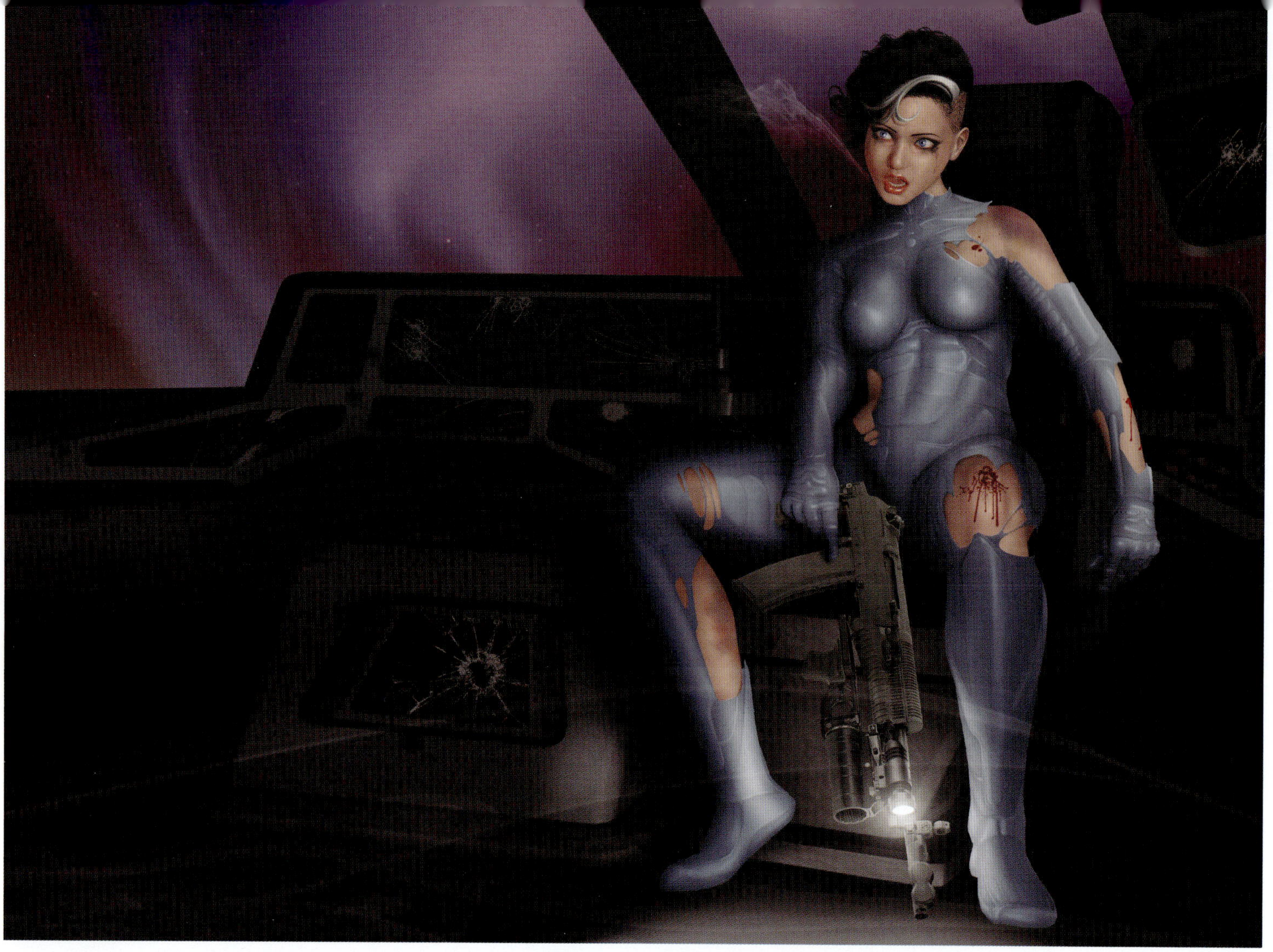

Untitled Space

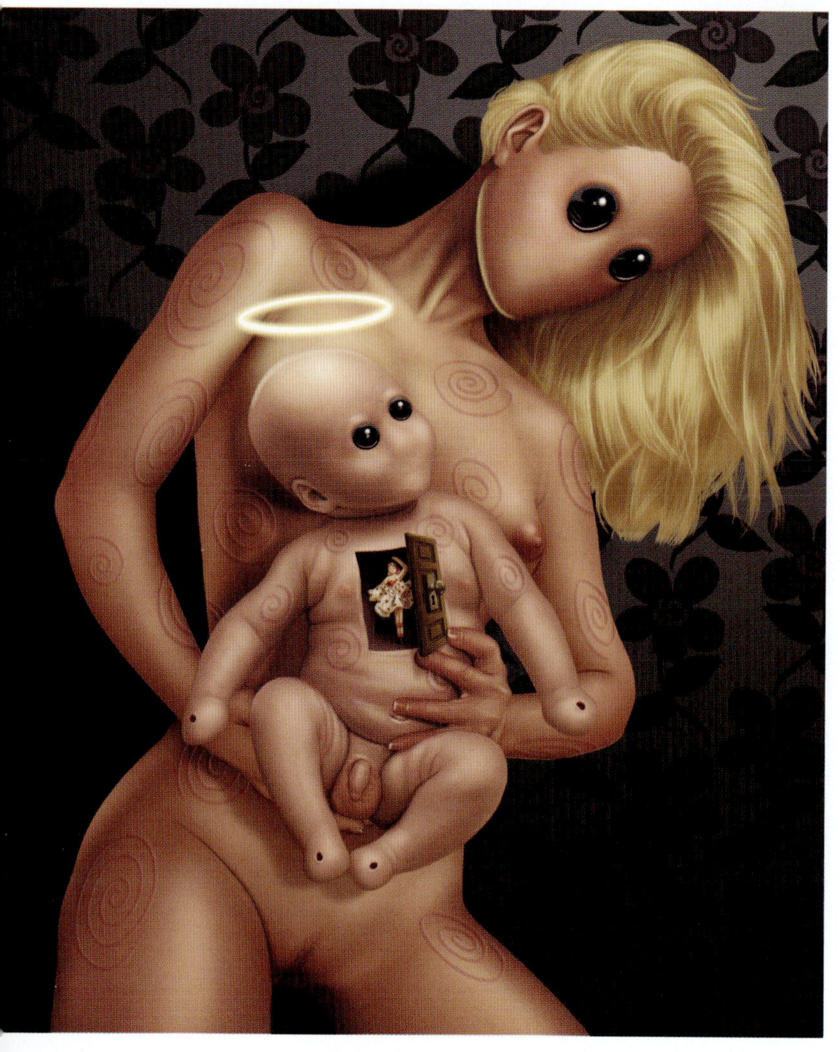

Baby Jesus Buttplug

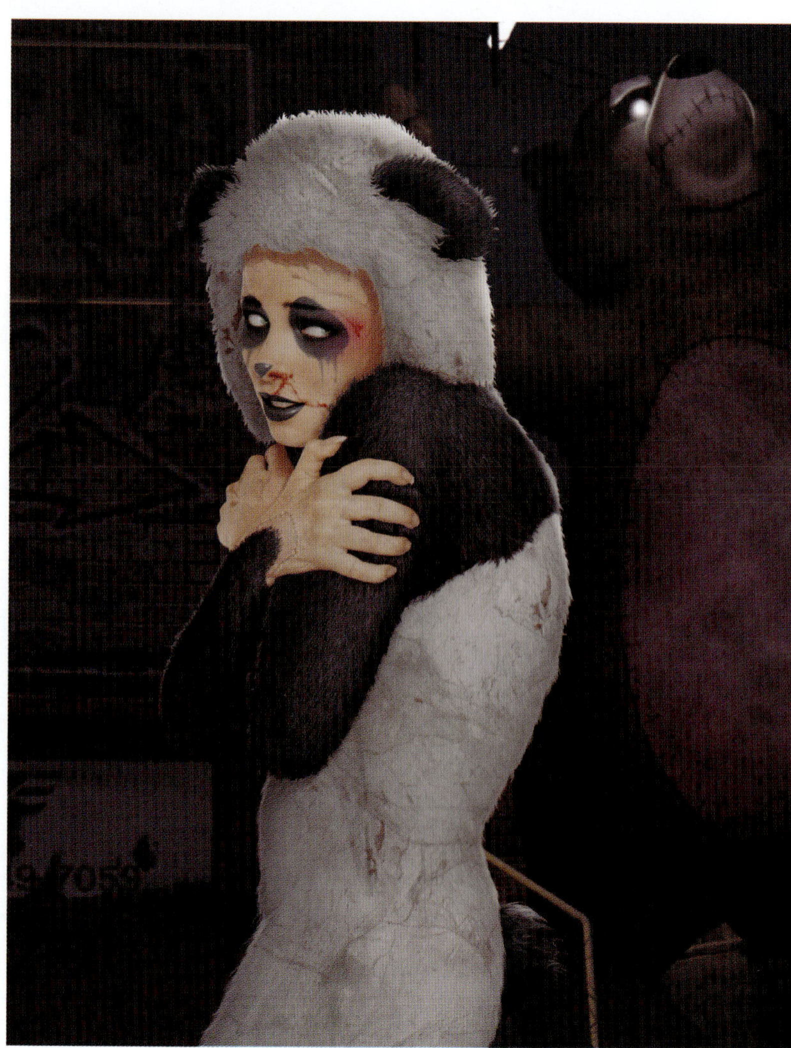

Cuddly Apocalypse

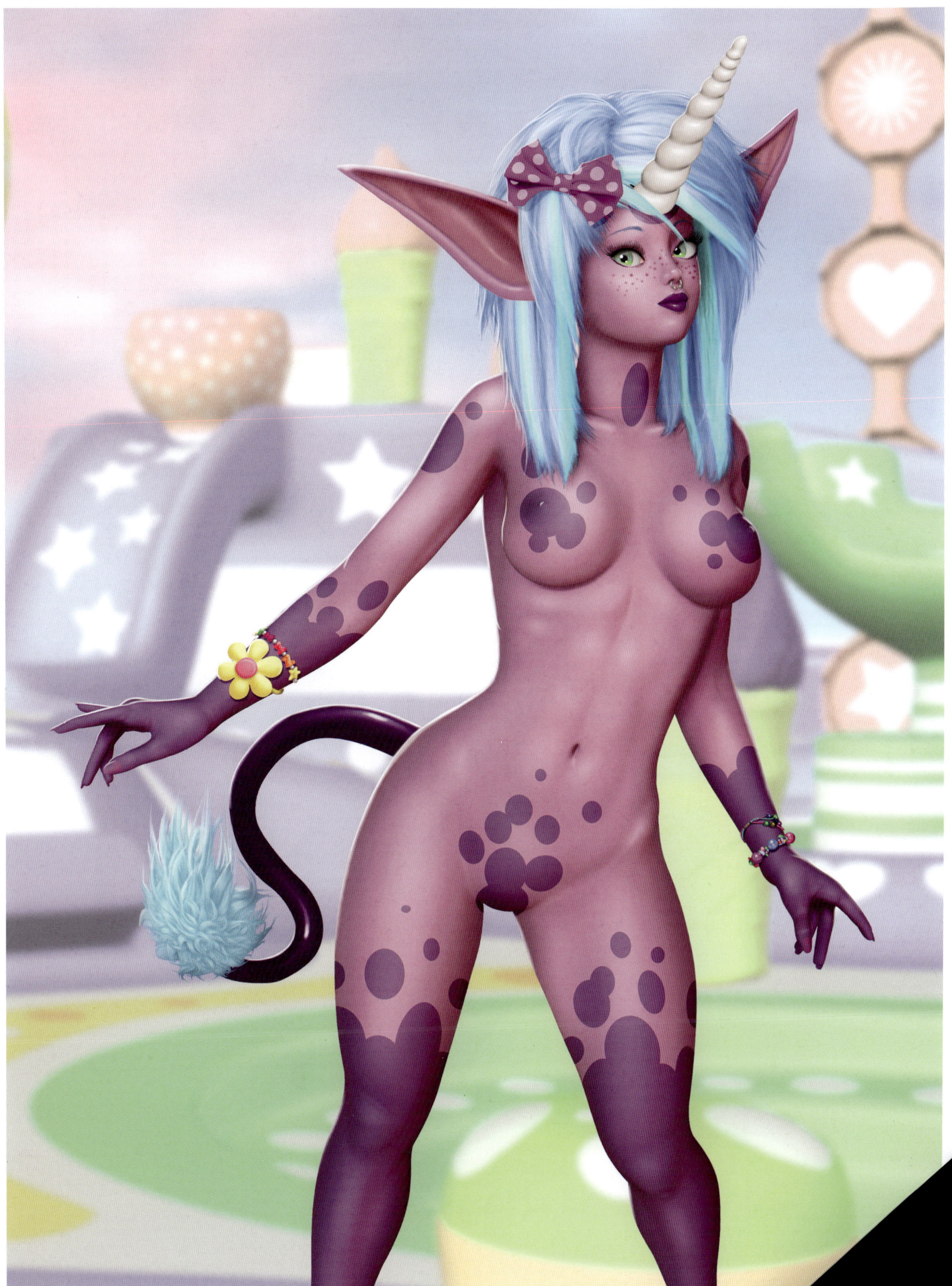

Super Cute

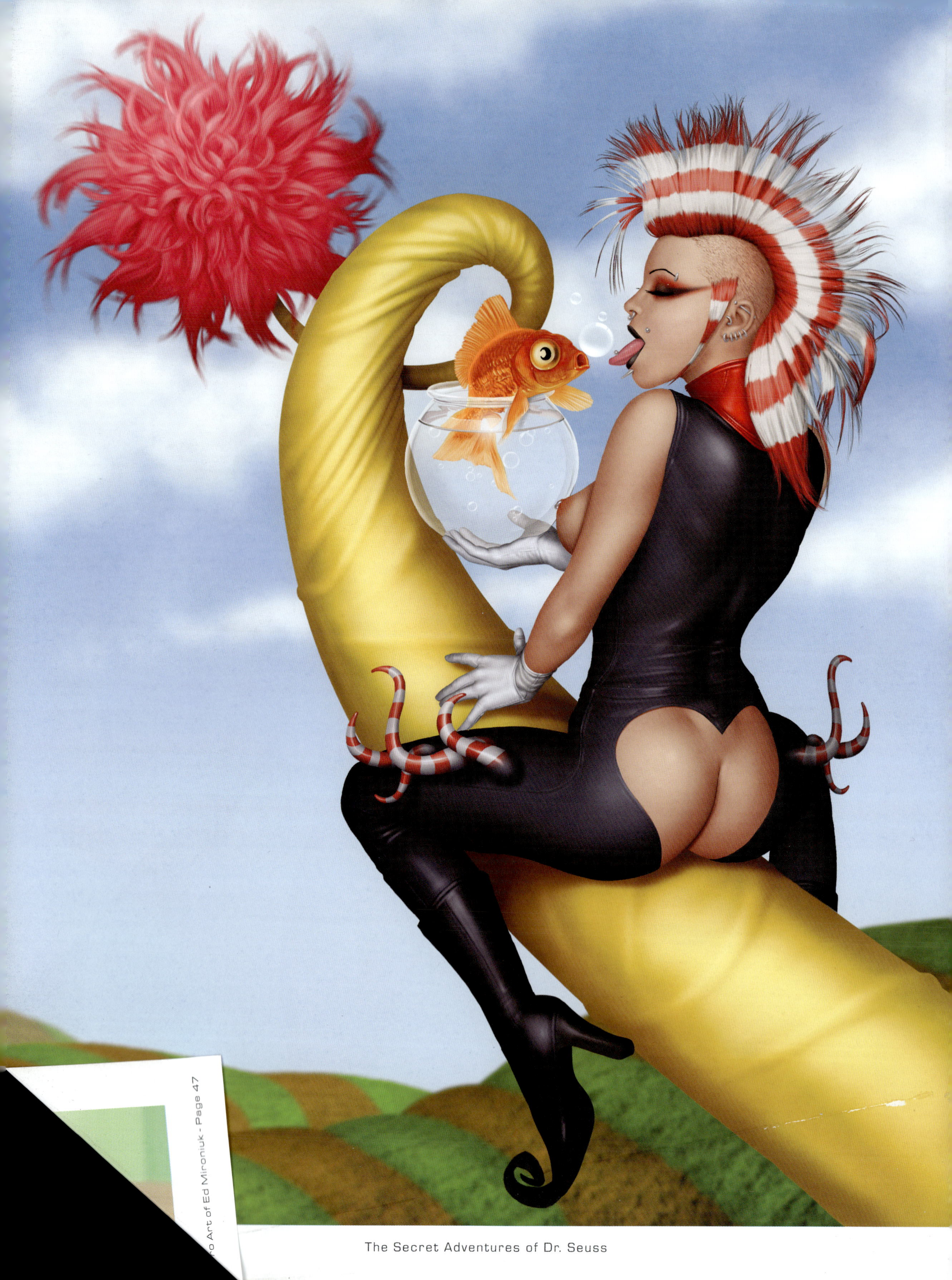

The Secret Adventures of Dr. Seuss